VIETNAMESE COOKERY

by

Jill Nhu Huong Miller

HERE, FOR THE FIRST TIME in English, is an absolutely authentic, definitive, and most distinctive collection of Vietnamese recipes.

Among the somewhat unusual and fascinating ingredients (available most anywhere) are such succulents as bamboo shoots, Chinese cabbage, mushrooms, water chestnuts, bean sprouts, coconut, pineapple, shrimp, and an interesting vermicelli called "bean threads" or "long rice." And when it comes to dried lily flowers, Chinese parsley, fresh mint leaves, and citronella root, the author tells you what to substitute if you do not have them, or simply to leave them out. All this is explained in a comprehensive ten-page glossary of special oriental foodstuff.

The basic ingredients, of course, are pork, chicken, beef, and everyday vegetables, but cooked and seasoned with a distinctive, pleasant, not-too-far-out flavor. Not until one tastes, for example, beef stew cooked with stick cinnamon, can one appreciate how good it is. Equally tasty is the caramelized pork, the stuffed and fried cucumbers, banana cake with cashews, and almond cookies second to none.

In order to preserve the texture, the taste, and the natural color of foods, particularly vegetables, many of these recipes call for sauteing them momentarily over sizzling hot heat.

The most distinctive element in Vietnamese cookery, however, is the extensive use of *Nuoc Mam Sauce* for seasoning, similar to the use made of soy sauce in Japanese and Chinese cookery. Like soy, it is very salty, but unlike soy it enhances and blends so subtly with other flavors that one can barely detect its presence and certainly would never suspect its being an extract of pickled fish. Instructions are given on how to mix it and where to obtain the makings.

Another distinctive feature of Vietnamese recipes, and particularly those in this book, is their adaptability to suit individual preferences. Also noteworthy throughout this book are the unusually detailed step-by-step instructions given by the author, and her constant concern over the elimination of disagreeable food odors.

The author, Jill Nhu Huong Miller, a native of Vietnam who has lived in all parts of the country, has had extensive experience in the fields of nursing, home economics, and dietetics. Presently she is serving the United States Armed Forces in Hawaii as a language instructor, for which she has received a Certificate of Achievement from Headquarters, 25th Infantry Division.

VIETNAMESE COOKERY

by
Jill Nhu Huong Miller

CHARLES E. TUTTLE COMPANY: PUBLISHERS
Rutland, Vermont
Tokyo, Japan

Representatives
Continental Europe: BOXERBOOKS, INC., *Zurich*
British Isles: PRENTICE-HALL INTERNATIONAL, INC., *London*
Australasia: BOOK WISE (AUSTRALIA) PTY. LTD.
104-108 Sussex Street, Sydney 2000

Published by the Charles E. Tuttle Company, Inc.
of Rutland, Vermont & Tokyo, Japan
with editorial offices at
Suido 1-chome, 2-6, Bunkyo-ku, Tokyo, Japan

Copyright in Japan, 1968, by Charles E. Tuttle Co., Inc.

Library of Congress Catalog Card No. 68-13869

International Standard Book No. 0-8048-1200-4

First edition, 1968
Sixth printing, 1986

PRINTED IN JAPAN

CONTENTS

To Terry Thompson
without whose help
this book would not have been written

FOREWORD

THE INITIAL IDEA for making the delicacies of Vietnamese cuisine available to the English speaking world through the medium of a housewives' cookbook evolved from many happy meals shared by myself and Mrs. Bernice Chang of Honolulu. Following her suggestion, I began to try to recall many of the tasty dishes of my homeland, and attempted to make a systematic record of them in the fond hope that they would someday be compiled, edited, and published for the benefit of others who wish to explore the great variety of Southeast Asian cooking. Without this original stimulus and continued encouragement of Mrs. Chang, the recipes of this book would probably have remained in my own kitchen, and shared only with my cherished guests.

Translating the cook's activities in the kitchen into the printed word is a major obstacle which anyone who tries to write a cook book must ultimately face. For the cook, the art in the kitchen usually comes much easier than the craft of describing her work on paper. For a Vietnamese to attempt this in English was almost enough to discourage the whole idea. Had it not been for the patience, dedication, and unstinted efforts of Mrs. Terry Thompson, this major obstacle may never have been overcome. Only through her careful observations in the kitchen, notations, editing, and typing of the manuscript have I been able to transmit my experiences in Vietnamese cookery to the English-speaking reader. With Terry, I have been privileged to share personally many of the dishes which are described in this book. It is only through her that I am now able to share them with you.

JILL NHU HUONG MILLER

VIETNAMESE COOKING

VIETNAMESE COOKING IS EASY. "Especially for Vietnamese housewives," you say? Nonsense. It can also be easy for non-Vietnamese housewives, and even for non-housewives. This book has fairly detailed instructions, with the idea that even a beginning cook (or one who has never even eaten oriental food) will be able to use it to make some typical, simple Vietnamese dishes. There are more complicated recipes, too, for the more experienced or more adventurous cook.

Vietnamese food has its own special character, as do most regional foods. Though it has been much influenced by Chinese cooking through many centuries, it still retains its own individuality. Chinese and Japanese food, especially, are often darker in color because of the extensive use of soy sauce for seasoning. Since fish sauce is used for seasoning in Vietnam, the food retains more of its natural color.

Indian, Malay, and French cooking have also had some slight influence on Vietnamese regional recipes, and Buddhist vegetarian cookery has been well-known there for a long time. The combination makes for an endless variety of dishes, and this book barely scratches the surface.

Before beginning to cook, read through the recipe to be sure you have all the ingredients (or substitutes). Many of the special ingredients may be omitted, and though the dish will be different, it will not necessarily be ruined. In each such case the ingredient is marked "optional." A few typical dishes that will probably be difficult to duplicate outside Vietnam have been included for interest.

Most of these recipes may be prepared with ingredients found fairly easily in any metropolitan area. The major ingredient appearing in almost every recipe, that will not be found on every supermarket shelf, is the fish sauce (Vietnamese *nuoc mam*). That, however, will be found on any Chinese or Philippine grocer's shelf and can be ordered by any gourmet shop. It is not particularly expensive.

Many of the more exotic ingredients may be found in any Chinese or other oriental grocery store, and many may be ordered from a Chinese grocer in a nearby metropolitan area if your town doesn't have one. Look for a Chinese restaurant and ask where to buy Chinese groceries in your area. Often the Chinese grocer will have a tiny, not well-advertised shop. Those who patronize him know where he is and he isn't in competition with the supermarket—he usually sells just those special ingredients not sold by other stores in the area. If you have your list in hand, he can bring out what you need. Part of the fun of trying some of these recipes is trying to track down some of the ingredients!

Happy cooking!

EQUIPMENT

ALMOST NO SPECIAL EQUIPMENT is needed for use with this cookbook. However, specific types of pans are better than others and a short description of the meaning of terms used in these recipes should be of use to the cook.

Mortar and Pestle: This is the only rather specialized equipment needed for Vietnamese cookery. Vietnamese women prefer to crush things; this brings out the flavor more than chopping or grinding. However, if you do not have a mortar and pestle and can't get one, you may chop or grind things. The texture and flavor will be different, but not offensively different. (Two exceptions: SHRIMP PASTE page 25 and FANCY BARBECUED PORK ON SKEWERS, page 42, *must* be pounded.)

To properly use a mortar and pestle, the pestle should be heavy enough to do a lot of the work for you. Wooden pestles are lighter in weight and easier to lift, but it takes more muscle power to do a proper job. Vietnamese pestles are normally made of stone, and the mortar is also of stone.

If you have a mortar and pestle, or can get one, try crushing things in small quantities to begin with, until you get the rhythm. Use your free hand to push things back down in the mortar, taking care not to smash any fingers.

Knives: Since much slicing and chopping is an essential part of Vietnamese cooking, good sharp knives are important. Especially useful is what is often called a French knife. It is about a foot long, including the handle, and the blade is usually about 3 inches wide at the end near the handle. It has a sharp point. This knife may be used for chopping, with a sort of rocking motion; it is good for slicing; and it may also be used for chopping through chicken and other light bones. It is a very versatile knife, though it may take a little practice to become accustomed to it.

Stainless steel knives do not usually have as sharp an edge and are more difficult to sharpen. A plain steel knife, which will probably rust and begin to look rather disreputable, but may be cleaned easily with ordinary pot scrubbers, is easy to sharpen and not expensive to replace. It is usually heavier, too, which means it is easier to use for chopping.

Smaller paring knives are also useful but no special kind is necessary.

Skillets: An iron skillet is always good for the type of cooking described in this book. It is heavy, does not scorch easily, and is easy to keep clean. Any good, heavy skillet will do. "Large" means a skillet larger than 10 inches across. A "medium" skillet is 8 to 10 inches across. Use what you have, and experiment to see which ones work best for you.

Pots: There are a few recipes in this book calling for a very large soup pot. Any type of pot will do, since it is the size that is most important. Other pots and pans may be of any type. New and special varieties are not necessary. Sometimes a 2-quart or 3-quart pot may be specified—just be sure you use one at least that big, or things will boil over. A larger pot may always be used, though if one too large for the job is used the liquid may cook away too fast.

Steamer: If you have a steamer, use it. If not, a substitute may be found. One type of substitute is a roasting pan with a cake rack (if the roaster does not have a rack). A large skillet, with a rack and a lid, may also be used. The major requirement for a steamer is that the food being steamed be surrounded by steam, under a cover that fits.

If a steamer is used, put several cups (depending on the size of the steamer) of water in the bottom section and bring to a boil on high heat. The top section will have holes in the bottom, and the food is either put directly on the bottom, or in a heat resistant bowl or pan, or wrapped in cloth, leaves, or aluminum foil. Such instructions are contained in the individual recipes. When the water in the bottom section is boiling, the top section with the food is set into place, the cover is put on, and the steaming begins. Be sure enough water remains in the bottom of the steamer so that there is plenty of steam.

INGREDIENTS

SINCE MANY OF THE INGREDIENTS used in ordinary Vietnamese cooking will seem exotic to the non-oriental cook, it seemed wise to include the following discussion of many of the ingredients. In many cases there are simple substitutes, and when an ingredient is seldom found outside Vietnam the substitute is usually used in the recipe. In many cases the more exotic ingredients may simply be omitted if not available.

alum: Used to make fruit firm when candying, so the fruit will not get mushy or disintegrate. Follow instructions in recipe.

bamboo shoots: Although fresh bamboo shoots are readily available in Vietnam, canned Chinese bamboo shoots are very good. Japanese canned bamboo shoots have a different flavor, intended for Japanese foods, and do not blend well with Vietnamese foods. Because of the shape of the shoot, slices will be quite irregular. *Substitute:* none.

bamboo shoots, dried: In Vietnam fresh bamboo shoots are available most of the year. Dried bamboo shoots are usually sun dried, by the housewife, for home use during the short season when fresh ones are not available. The dried bamboo shoots that are found in oriental groceries outside the orient are usually kiln dried for much longer storage and consequently must be soaked and cooked for a longer period. *Substitute:* fresh or canned bamboo shoots may be substituted for dried ones in any recipe. The flavor will be slightly different.

banana: Bananas are plentiful, in numerous varieties, in Vietnam. The recipes using bananas in this book are for the most ordinary bananas that are available throughout the world.

banana leaf: Banana leaves are often used to wrap foods for steaming, because of the enormous size, the firm texture that does not allow the leaf to disintegrate during cooking, and the lack of distinctive flavor to transfer to the food being cooked. *Substitutes:* ti leaf is a good substitute, but is not much more available than banana leaves in many parts of the world. A more readily available substitute is a close-woven cloth, such as a tea-towel, or several layers of cheesecloth, usually oiled.

beans, green: In Vietnamese quick-fried foods, green beans are delicious if used fresh. Frozen beans are much softer when cooked, and do not have the slightly crunchy texture of the fresh beans. If you prefer softer beans, by all means use frozen ones. Canned green beans may also be used, but the flavor is less desirable and the texture will be soft instead of crunchy. Green beans are usually sliced in what is known in English as "French cut"—which might also be called "Vietnamese cut"!

bean curd, also known as *dofu* in some Chinese dialects and *tofu* in Japanese: This is a curd made from the soy bean. It is normally made fresh every day, and keeps only a few days under refrigeration. It has very little flavor of its own, but absorbs the flavor of foods it is cooked with. It is sometimes available canned, and will be found in either Japanese or Chinese groceries. *Substitute:* none. Omit if not available, and not a part of the title of the recipe.

bean sauce: Chinese bean sauce is an ingredient of one or two recipes in this book. It comes in a can, and can be ordered from a specialty grocer if not found any other place. Normally sold in all Chinese groceries. Has a rather strong, distinctive flavor. *Substitute:* none. May usually be omitted.

bean sprouts: These are produced by immersing dried beans of a special variety in water. The water temperature is controlled so that the beans put out sprouts just as they would if planted. They are particularly popular in the orient. The flavor is delicate, though distinctive (pleasantly so), and the texture is tender but crunchy. They may be used to good effect in a tossed salad, just as they come or blanched for a minute or so. To keep in the refrigerator, put into a container and cover with cool water. Change the water every couple of days and they will remain fresh-tasting about a week. Do not cover. Canned bean sprouts are also available. These should be drained and rinsed thoroughly under cool running water before use. *Substitute:* none. May be omitted from many of the recipes.

bean thread, often called "long rice": This resembles vermicelli in shape, but the texture is quite different and unlike any other type of noodle or pasta. It is almost crunchy after being soaked in water. It looks much like strings of cellophane. It is normally sold in 2-ounce packages, tied with string and covered with cellophane. Must be soaked in warm water before using. *Substitute:* none. May often simply be omitted.

bitter melon: A small melon, with very bumpy surface much like some decorative varieties of gourd or squash. It is pale green and has a bitter flavor. Much used in the orient, it should not be used as the main part of a meal—a little goes a long way, but it does make a pleasing contrast with an otherwise bland meal. *Substitute:* none.

borax: It took quite a search to discover the English translation of this item, which was finally furnished by Mr. Nguyen van Hung, an Architecture student at the University of Washington. It is used in rinsing shrimp. to remove the fishy odor, help clean it, and to make the meat firmer. The shrimp must be thoroughly washed after soaking a few minutes in a mild borax solution.

cabbage: When "cabbage" is specified in one of these recipes, ordinary white head cabbage is meant. It may be substituted for Chinese cabbage, but the flavor will be different. It is usually cooked only a short time to avoid the unpleasant odor that develops from long contact with heat.

cabbage, Chinese, also known as *bok choy:* Chinese cabbage has become fairly popular in the United States in recent years as a salad vegetable. It is also delicious when cooked for a short time with fresh pork or other delicacies. This type of cabbage is leafy, not headed, long in shape, and has crinkled edges on the leaves. The stem portion is white, and the leaves are whitish to pale green. *Substitute:* ordinary head cabbage may be substituted, with a slight change in flavor.

cabbage, mustard, also called *kai choy:* Mustard cabbage is not usually available in places without a large oriental population. It is similar to Chinese cabbage, except the stem portion of the leaf is green instead of white. *Substitute:* young turnip greens, including tiny young turnips. The flavor will be different, but good.

chili pepper: The small red (or green) hot pepper is used in many ways in Southeast Asia. It may be added in any desired quantity, when specified. This collection does not include very many of the really hot dishes of Vietnam. It is usually crushed, because that brings out the flavor better. It may be served as a side dish with almost any Vietnamese food.

Chinese cabbage, see *cabbage, Chinese*

Chinese parsley: A pungent herb, used fresh as a garnish in many Vietnamese dishes. It has a distinctly different flavor, so there is no real substitute, though ordinary parsley may be eaten instead. It should be used in moderation, with extra amounts offered for individual taste, since a few people are not fond of the flavor while others like a lot of it. May be omitted, if not available.

Chinese peas: This delicacy is widely used in the orient. The pea pod is served whole, before the peas have begun to mature while it is still very sweet and tender. The shape is similar to the pod of a lima bean or a green pea, but it is extremely flat and about ½ inch wide. Some large grocers now have packages of frozen Chinese peas. *Substitute:* French cut green beans. Fresh beans, cut in the French fashion, are sweeter and better, but frozen ones are acceptable.

Chinese sausage: A small sausage, rather sweet, made of seasoned pork and pork fat. It may be steamed on top of rice, then sliced into angled rounds, or it may be sliced and fried or added to numerous other dishes. Since it is dried, it may be shipped and refrigerated, so it may be possible to order it if it is not locally available. There are manufacturers both in Canada and in the United States. *Substitute:* mild, sweetish sausage may be substituted, but hot or strong-flavored sausages will give an entirely different effect. There is no real equivalent; as with all sausages, the unique combination of flavors is inherent.

Chinese winter melon, see *winter melon*

Chinese yam, also called "chop suey yam": This is a starchy root vegetable, light brown, with a rather flattened, fat, and scalloped shape. *Substitute:* kohlrabi.

cinnamon: Stick cinnamon is used frequently in Vietnamese stew or soup. It has a different effect from powdered cinnamon, which may be substituted in a pinch, ½ tsp. powdered cinnamon for ½ a stick of cinnamon.

citronella root, also known as "lemon grass": Fresh citronella is readily available in Vietnam and in Hawaii, though it may not be available outside other metropolitan areas unless grown in the home garden. It is an attractive, foot-high, grasslike plant that clumps and multiplies rapidly. The edible portion is the lower part of the stem, before the grasslike leaf begins. When sliced in thin rounds it is similar in shape to the white portion of a green onion, though much firmer in texture and very different in flavor. It has a pungent, pleasant odor, and a very distinctive flavor, usually well liked by foreigners as well as by Vietnamese. Also known as "lemon grass" in some parts of Asia, it is sometimes available in powdered form in metropolitan areas, usually imported from Holland (a result of Indonesian influence). Some gourmet shops will try to order the powdered lemon grass for you. *Substitute:* 3 thin slices of fresh ginger root, or onion, if so specified in the recipe. For most recipes in this book, it may simply be omitted if not a part of the name of the dish.

coconut, dried: Dried shredded, bakers' coconut may often be substituted for fresh coconut in these recipes, particularly in the desserts. In some of the other recipes it is not such a satisfactory substitute because it has been sweetened and adds a sweet flavor that does not combine well with the other ingredients.

coconut, fresh: There are plenty of fresh coconuts in Vietnam, and many recipes for Vietnamese dishes include coconut milk or coconut water or grated (or shredded) fresh coconut. Only a sampling of these recipes is included in this book, since fresh coconuts are not so available outside tropical areas.

In buying fresh coconut, be sure there is still plenty of water inside: shake it and listen. If you are able to get a really fresh coconut, you are faced with removing the thick, football-shaped (and sized) outer husk, first. This is best done with an ordinary garden pick. Push one end of the pick firmly into the ground, leaving the pointed end up. Push the side of the coconut husk against the point, pulling away sideways at the same time. Continue all the way around until the coconut is husked. The outer husk is filled with a type of fiber which is used in many parts of the world to make a very sturdy rope or string.

Then comes the opening of the inner shell—the part that is most often seen outside tropical and semitropical areas. There are three "eyes" near one end of the coconut. If you take a small flat stone, or a small hammer, and tap the coconut about its middle, just under the eyes, it will crack. Continue tapping around the middle, gently but firmly, and it will break cleanly in half. The break is not from point to point, but around the middle.

Now to get at the meat. A heavy screwdriver is the best implement for this. A sharp-pointed knife is not so good—the point often breaks off and it simply does not work as well. The meat will have a brown skin that comes off the shell. This should be peeled away before using the meat. The juice that is in the middle of the coconut is not, contrary to popular misconception, the coconut milk. It is juice, or water, discussed below.

coconut juice, or coconut water: Many people think the liquid inside the fresh coconut is the coconut milk referred to in these recipes. Actually, the liquid rattling around inside the coconut is coconut juice or coconut water, and is sometimes used in recipes but more often is used as a nourishing cool drink, just as it comes from the coconut. One famous recipe using the juice of green coconuts is included. *Substitute:* none.

coconut milk: The "milk" of a coconut is made by grating fresh coconut very fine, then squeezing the grated meat. The liquid that runs out is white and milky looking, and is used in many tropical countries as a basic cooking ingredient or sauce. For instructions on making coconut milk, see page 26. *Substitute:* heavy cream, about 3 tablespoons cream for ½ cup coconut milk, since the cream is much oilier.

cornstarch: Used in many of these recipes, cornstarch slightly thickens juice or soup. Flour may be substituted in an emergency, but the texture, flavor and total effect will be different.

dried foods: see the specific name, e.g., *mushrooms, lily flowers, shrimp,* etc.

eggplant: There is a type of eggplant shaped more like a cucumber except longer and thinner. This, if available, is preferred for Vietnamese recipes. The more common, fat and round eggplant is an acceptable substitute. The color of both varieties is the same.

fish sauce, also known as "fish's gravy," the English name used on bottled Chinese fish sauce; and as *patis,* the Philippine version of the same sauce. This fish sauce is the Vietnamese equivalent of salt, or of soy sauce in many other oriental recipes. It is almost clear, with a slight yellowish tint, and has a very fishy odor. When used in moderation, as in these recipes, it adds a subtle and very agreeable bit of flavor.

The Vietnamese fish sauce has received very bad publicity in recent years because of the wide use of poor quality fish sauce in Vietnam during the extended period of war and turmoil. Buy good quality fish sauce, which is quite a different thing.

Fish sauce is made by packing fresh fish in barrels, in layers alternating with layers of salt, and allowing the fish and salt to ferment. The fermented, very salty, sauce is then drained off, processed and bottled. Second rate sauce is made by pressing the fish after the first quality sauce has been drained off. Even poorer quality sauce is made by adding water and pressing. Buy the best! It is available at any Chinese grocer, since it is also widely used in some types of Chinese cooking. It may also be available in places where Philippine foods are sold. Any gourmet shop should be able to order it easily.

Substitute: none. Fish sauce is what makes Vietnamese food uniquely Vietnamese. Additional salt may be added, if it is absolutely unavailable, but the dish will be only a substitute for Vietnamese cookery.

flour: Several varieties of flour are used in the recipes in this book, and unless otherwise specified regular wheat flour is called simply "flour." Rice flour and glutinous rice flour are ingredients in several of the hors d'oeuvre and dessert recipes, and will be readily available in almost any oriental grocery and may be found in many specialty shops. Potato flour has been found to be a very acceptable substitute for manioc (tapioca) flour, which is used in Vietnam, so has been included in the recipes which originally used manioc flour.

ginger root: Fresh ginger root is a well-known part of all oriental cookery. It is used for flavor, for calming down the slightly objectionable odor of boiling chicken, for an aid to the digestion—it has many uses that are only touched upon in this book. Powdered ginger is not a substitute. If fresh ginger root is not available, it can be omitted or (if specified in the particular recipe) green onion may sometimes be substituted. Dried whole ginger root, incidentally, is now quite generally available and can be reconstituted by soaking in warm water to cover for several hours or overnight.

glutinous rice: see *rice, glutinous*

green onion: see *onion*

leeks: A leek is similar in shape to a green onion, except it is several times larger and stronger in flavor. Pickled leeks, the only type used in these recipes, may be found in specialty shops and will be available from almost any oriental grocer. *Substitute:* pickled onions that are not too sweet.

lemon grass, see *citronella root*

lily flowers, dried: These flowers are usually sun dried in the orient. Those exported for sale in oriental groceries are usually kiln dried. The flower looks like a pale brown strip of root, or of leather, from 3 to 4 inches long. It must be soaked in warm water 10 to 15 minutes to soften, then the hard stem-end should be pinched off and discarded. In some recipes the flowers will be chopped, but often you will be told to tie each flower in a knot. The knot makes a slight crunch when eaten, giving variation to the texture of the dish. The flavor is very mild and pleasant. *Substitute:* none. May be omitted without serious results, unless "lily flowers" occurs in the name of the dish.

long rice, see *bean thread* and *noodles* (py mei fun)

look fun, see *noodles,* look fun

lotus root: This oriental staple food is a mild-flavored root vegetable related to the tubers. It is long and rather fat, about the size of a toy baseball bat or smaller, with a light, brownish-white color. It has holes running from top to bottom inside, so that when it is sliced in rounds it looks something like Swiss cheese. Only one recipe using lotus root is included in this book. *Substitute:* none.

mint: Fresh mint leaves may be used as a garnish with most Vietnamese foods, or as a side dish or salad with leaf lettuce and Chinese parsley. In Vietnam there are several varieties of mint, but any fresh mint adds a sparkle to the meal. Especially good in a green tossed salad.

monosodium glutamate: Often called "taste powder," and also sold under the Japanese name of *Aji-no-moto,* this condiment is used sparingly in some of the recipes.

mushrooms, dried: Dried mushrooms have quite a different taste from fresh ones, and are used in much oriental cookery. This makes them easily available from specialty shops and oriental groceries. The ordinary dried mushrooms are fairly large, from 2 to 4 or more inches across. There are also what are sometimes called "perfumed mushrooms" which are not used in these recipes.

Dried mushrooms must be soaked for 10 minutes or so in warm water before using. The hard part of the stem is then cut away, and is often discarded though it may be added to long-cooking soup or stew for flavor. Since the size varies considerably, the quantity called for in these recipes is only approximate. Because mushrooms have a delicate flavor, the quantity may be varied considerably with no disservice to the dish. And since the flavor is pleasant, and mushrooms have little caloric value, dieters might consider their use for variety. *Substitute:* fresh mushrooms may be substituted, though the flavor and texture is quite different. May be omitted, unless "mushroom" is a part of the name of the recipe.

mushrooms, fresh: When fresh mushrooms are called for, the best type to use is the large, brown variety. The smaller button mushrooms may be substituted, and may be specified in some recipes. In some recipes canned button mushrooms may be substituted. Japanese canned mushrooms have the wrong flavor, one meant for combination with Japanese seasonings, and should not be used in these recipes.

mushrooms, straw: "Straw" mushrooms are a delicacy usually found only in Chinese groceries. Very delicate flavor, slightly larger than button mushrooms. *Substitute:* fresh (not canned) button mushrooms.

ngun si fun, see *noodles*

no mai, see *rice, glutinous*

noodles, look fun (the Chinese name): These are rice noodles, and in places with a large Chinese population you may be able to find the fresh ones. If so, by all means try them. In fact, try them fresh, warmed in a steamer and sliced in half-inch wide strips, dipped in Nuoc Mam Sauce (page 23), with a little lettuce or other green salad, Delicious! The substitution of dried noodles for fresh ones is similar to the substitution of powdered milk for fresh milk. Good, but not the same.

These noodles are available dried, in packages, but be careful about the instructions printed on the package. Some manufacturers print poor or wrong instructions! Soak the dried noodles at least two hours, in warm water to cover. Then boil about 5 minutes, or until tender all the way through. Drain, slice into ½ or ¼ inch strips or as directed in the recipe. If boiled too long, the noodles will disintegrate. *Substitute:* wide egg, wheat, or other noodles. The flavor will be different, but the idea will be similar.

noodles, py mei fun (or *ngun si fun*) (Chinese rice sticks): These are very fine, extremely delicate and tender rice noodles. They are packed in thumb-sized bundles each tied with string. After soaking for a few minutes, the string may be untied gently. Then soak an additional 15 minutes or so. Bring just to the boiling point and drain immediately. These noodles disintegrate easily into rice-grain sized pieces. Available at any Chinese grocery. *Substitute:* none.

noodles, sha ho fun (Chinese): Follow the instructions given under *noodles, look fun.*

noodles, somen (Japanese name): A type of Japanese wheat noodles, very thin and fine. *Substitute:* fine vermicelli.

onion: Use either white or yellow bulb-shaped cooking onions when "onion" is called for. May sometimes be substituted for green onion or for shallot, but with slightly changed flavor.

onion, green: Green onion is used in many of these recipes. Use part of the green top portion, too, for color as well as flavor. The green top is often used when boiling chicken, shrimp or pork to counteract the slightly offensive odor. *Substitute:* white or yellow cooking onion, or shallots, with a slight change in flavor.

papaya: A favorite fruit in most tropical areas, there are many varieties in Vietnam. It is good served ripe, with a wedge of lemon or lime. When green, it is very firm and a bright dark green in color. It turns gold as it ripens and begins to get slightly less firm. *Substitute:* none.

peanuts: Unless otherwise specified, regular salted, roasted peanuts may be used in these recipes. Chopped peanuts are often used as a garnish. If chopped, be sure to use the "dust" also, since much of the good flavor and odor is there.

pineapple: Fresh pineapple is called for in several of these recipes, and is often used in cooking as a vegetable in Vietnam. As a result, sweetened canned pineapple is not a very satisfactory substitute. Unsweetened canned pineapple is available in some specialty shops, and may be substituted.

py mei fun, see *noodles*

rice: The usual long-grain rice is not used too often in the orient—it is considered quite a luxury. It also has less flavor, because it has been refined so much. If you can shop at an oriental grocery, ask for ordinary rice or short-grain rice—it is much shorter in price, usually, too! Much of it is grown in California. Long grain rice may be used, but it is harder to eat with chopsticks. Instant rice is not really acceptable.

rice, glutinous, also called *no mai:* This is a special kind of rice, used in very special dishes. It is available in oriental groceries. *Substitute:* none.

rice, roasted: Toast regular rice in a small covered skillet on top of the stove, shaking constantly, until dark brown, being careful not to burn it. May be stored, but it is only used in one recipe in this book so just toast the small amount needed.

rice flour: There are several kinds of rice flour, most of which will be readily available at an oriental grocery and probably at many specialty shops. There are a few recipes for hors d'oeuvres and desserts calling for rice flour and the specific type will be described in the recipe. *Substitute: none.*

rice paper: A very special Vietnamese food, with no real substitute except perhaps the Greek *philo.* It is a tissue-paper thin round sheet of dried rice paste, which is sturdy enough to be used for wrapping things in a roll after it is dampened and softened with water. It is very popular in Vietnam, but is not ordinarily available outside that country. *Substitute:* none. Leaf lettuce or cabbage leaves can be used in some cases as wrappers, but the flavor and texture will not be the same.

rice wine: Use Chinese rice wine, dry sherry or dry sauterne. Rum or brandy in smaller quantity may also be substituted. Japanese rice wine—sake—is too mild.

saffron: This is what gives the warm, golden color to curry. It is also used as a dye. The root of the saffron plant is dried, and crushed just before using, in Vietnam. Powdered saffron loses its strength easily, especially if exposed to light. Sometimes the addition of a pinch or two of paprika will help give a warmer color. Saffron also has a delicate flavor. *Substitute:* in some recipes, the substitution of curry powder is recommended. Otherwise, omit if not available.

sausage, see *Chinese sausage*

sesame seeds: A real must as a garnish for many Vietnamese dishes, these tiny seeds must be roasted and crushed a short time before using. To roast, use a small pan with a cover; the seeds will jump like popcorn when they get hot, though they don't puff up. Put over medium high heat and shake occasionally. Watch closely to be sure they don't burn. When beginning to turn a light golden brown remove from the heat and put in another container immediately to stop the roasting process. Partially crush the seeds with a mortar and pestle to bring out the aroma and flavor, just before using. A wonderful addition to tossed salads.

sha ho fun, see *noodles*

shallots: These are much used in Vietnamese cooking. When not available, substitute the white part of a green onion.

shrimp, dried: Tiny shrimp are kiln dried for use as a flavoring in many oriental recipes. The smaller the shrimp, the greater the delicacy. When called for in this book, they are always optional since non-oriental palates often find both the flavor and the odor objectionable. If you want to try them, try a very small quantity (smaller than called for in the recipe) at first. If you like them, add more! The shrimp are usually soaked 10 minutes or more in warm water before being added to the dish being cooked. Sometimes they are chopped after soaking. The soaking water is often added to soups. *Substitute:* fresh shrimp; or a dash of monosodium glutamate. The shrimp has the same effect as monosodium glutamate of heightening the flavor of other foods, as well as having a decided flavor of its own.

shrimp sauce (Chinese *harm ha*): To be found in oriental groceries; there is no real substitute. May be omitted, unless specifically told not to omit in the recipe. It has many of the same properties of dried shrimp. *Substitute:* a pinch of monosodium glutamate and ½ teaspoon salt for each teaspoon of shrimp sauce, to heighten the flavor, one of the reasons for using shrimp sauce.

somen, see *noodles*

soybean curd, see *bean curd*

squash, see *kwa:* Chinese squash, *Substitute:* zucchini squash.

squid: A type of seafood, related to octopus, with small tentacles. *Substitute:* none.

star fruit also called *star apple* or *carambole:* A kind of fruit, sometimes found as an ornamental plant in private gardens. When sliced across, the fruit has the shape of a star. *Substitute:* no real substitute, although in PORK-RIND SALAD (page 95), a lime-soaked cucumber substitute is given.

ti leaf (pronounced "tea"): Sometimes used to wrap foods or to line the top of the steamer. *Substitute:* Banana leaf, or oiled, firmly woven cloth, such as a tea towel.
tomato: Unless being used as a showpiece, as in STUFFED TOMATOES page 51, lower grade, cheaper cooking tomatoes may be used. If fresh tomatoes are out of season, well-drained canned tomatoes may be substituted with the usual deterioration of flavor.

tomato paste: Use Spanish style tomato paste, if available. The seasoning is more compatible with Vietnamese seasonings than is the Italian style.

tree fungus, dried: Dried tree fungus resembles thin, black dried mushrooms. They must be soaked in hot water, from 15 minutes to an hour, to be softened (depending on the recipe). Any black specks or stem portions, where the fungus grew on the tree, should be cut away. This staple can usually be found at any Chinese grocery, and if not available may be omitted without disaster to the recipe unless it is specifically a part of the name of the dish. It has little flavor, but a very unusual crisp, chewy texture that makes a pleasant contrast.

water chestnuts: A root vegetable, with a very crisp texture, and a very mild, slightly sweet flavor. Fresh water chestnuts (about the size of walnuts) must be peeled before using; canned ones may be used direct from the can. Delicious when added to a tossed salad. *Substitute:* none. Canned water chestnuts are widely distributed now.

wine, see *rice wine*

winter melon: A very tender-meated variety of gourd or squash. *Substitute:* butternut squash. Use a smaller quantity and cook 1 or 2 minutes longer.

yam, see *Chinese yam*

BASIC RECIPES

THERE ARE A FEW recipes that do not fit into any of the other chapters and that are basic to Vietnamese cooking. These have been gathered into this chapter.

COOKED RICE
Four servings

If you have an automatic, electric rice cooker, follow the simple directions that come with it. If you do not have one, and have never learned to cook rice in the oriental way, be sure to try this recipe. It is quick and very simple. Notice that there is no salt or other seasoning added. When cooked this way, the rice has a gentle but very nice flavor of its own. In the orient, rice is not normally eaten alone, but has something put on top of it. The things you serve with it, usually placed on top of the rice in a rice bowl for each individual, will give the rice all the seasoning it needs. Minute rice is in a different category; don't bother to try it with this recipe.

Heavy 4-qt. pot with lid
2 cups rice
1½ cups cool water

Wash the rice 2 or 3 times in cool tap water, changing the water each time and rubbing gently between the hands. The last water should be fairly clear. This will remove much of the starch covering the outside of the rice and will keep it from being too sticky. If highly refined rice is used it will need less rinsing and rubbing. Put the rice in a heavy pot and add water. Cover the pot and place on high heat until it boils. Watch carefully to be sure it doesn't boil over. Cook, covered, over high heat about 5 minutes. Lift the lid, and if you can't see much, or any, water over the top of the rice, and little holes appear in in the surface, remove it from the heat. Leave the high heat turned on, so it will be really hot when you return the rice to the burner. Drain the remaining water off the rice, and return it to the burner. Cover, and turn heat to the lowest setting. Let the rice sit on the heat, covered, from 20 to 30 minutes. Resist the temptation to uncover it and peek—that lets the steam escape and the rice may end up being too hard. Do not stir at all after it begins to cook, or it will probably get mushy.

The rice should be soft, but firm, and the grains should stick together enough to be picked up comfortably with chopsticks. Western-style cooked rice, with each grain fluffy and determinedly separate, is very hard to eat with chopsticks.

If you find that the rice in the very botton is slightly stuck to the pot, and slightly hard, cherish it! This is a delicacy. Eat it with any juice from meat dishes, etc. Vietnamese children beg for it.

POT ROASTED RICE   *Four servings*

This recipe for rice results in a true delicacy, the Vietnamese version of a type of rice cooked in many parts of Asia and the Near East. The Vietnamese often use pork fat or cooking oil instead of butter. Butter gives a delicate flavor that is very pleasant, but the other ways of cooking are also very good. This is good eaten alone, or with NUOC MAM SAUCE (page 23). It is usually cooked to accompany TOMATO-FRIED CHICKEN (page 81), but you will find it is good with almost any main dish. It is also the basic ingredient for a simple home-style meal of leftovers as described in the recipe on page 85 for MANY-COLORED CHICKEN FRIED RICE.

2 cups rice	Wash the rice thoroughly, then drain in a strainer or colander until almost completely dry again.
2 tbsp. butter (or pork fat or cooking oil) *Heavy skillet*	Melt the butter in the skillet on medium heat. Add rice and saute, stirring gently with a spatula or a spoon, for about 15 minutes on medium or medium high heat. The rice will begin to change color, the individual grains becoming whiter and more opaque and the panful of rice beginning to take on a faint golden tinge from a distance. Some grains of rice will begin to turn a golden brown around the edges.
1¾ cups hot water *Heavy pot with lid*	Pour the rice into the heavy pot, and add about 1¾ cups water. The water should cover the rice completely, and stand above the level of the rice about ¼ inch. Cover the pot, turn on high heat. If it boils over, remove from the heat; your pot is not big enough or not heavy enough, or perhaps both! After about 4 or 5 minutes, check the water, which should no longer be visible. Stir rice with chopsticks, or a fork, gently, from the bottom up, to fluff it. Do not stir very much. Cover the pot, and turn the heat to low. Continue to cook about 15 or 20 minutes, or until done. The rice should be tender, but may still be slightly chewy and will stick together enough to be eaten with chopsticks. Individual tastes differ. Some people prefer softer rice, and will need to add another ¼ cup of water. Others prefer a dryer rice, and may add ¼ cup less water. Keep warm until served. It may be steamed to reheat as a leftover.
TO SERVE	Serve as regular steamed or boiled rice, but plan to serve more per person!

TEA

Making tea is easy. Any kind of tea is all right, but Chinese tea or jasmine tea is preferable. Tea is not sweetened, creamed, or lemoned in Vietnam—unless "foreign" tea is being served. It is often served warm or cool, sometimes with ice, in a large glass. When served hot, especially to a guest, a cup is used.

Teapot *Hot water*	Use any size teapot. Experimentation will show you the size you need. A deodorized coffee pot may be used for larger quantities. Pour hot water into the pot and let it sit for a few minutes, to warm the pot. Discard the water.

1 tbsp. tea leaves	Put the tea leaves in the bottom of the pot. Pour the boiling water over the leaves and let it steep for about 5 minutes. Pour out into glasses, and let the tea cool off in the glass until it is easy to hold in the hand. Or if iced tea is preferred, add ice when the tea has cooled off.
1 qt. boiling water	

Additional tea may be made by pouring more boiling water over the same tea leaves, letting it steep slightly longer, but do not stir it.

NUOC MAM SAUCE

Nuoc mam is to Vietnamese cooking what salt is to cooking in the Western world. And the prepared nuoc mam sauce is a basic seasoning for numerous dishes. The quantity given here is small, enough for one or two meals for those who are just experimenting. For those who like the flavor, all quantities may be multiplied by four, or ten, or whatever number is desired. Don't believe all you hear about nuoc mam—it is delicious when prepared correctly and used in moderation.

Mortar and pestle (Page 9)	Seed the chili pepper. If you are not sure how hot you want this, start with a very little. It is easy to add more. Peel the garlic clove. Crush the pepper and garlic together in a mortar with the sugar. Peel and seed the lime and mash the pulp in the mortar with the garlic and pepper.
3 ¼-inch pieces fresh hot chili pepper	
1 garlic clove	
1 tsp. sugar	
½ medium lime	
1 tbsp. vinegar	Add vinegar and water to pulp mixture and mix well.
1 tbsp. water	
4 tbsp. fish sauce	Add the fish sauce (plain *nuoc mam*) last. If it is added before other ingredients the pieces of garlic, pepper, and lime pulp will all sink to the bottom, and it is much preferable to have them in suspension or floating on top.

This sauce can be used as soon as it is mixed, but it can also be kept for two or three months in the refrigerator. Store in a tightly closed bottle or jar.

BOILED PORK

Buy fresh ham for boiling, since it has less fat. A good lean piece is best. A green onion will counteract the slight odor of boiling pork.

1 lb. lean pork	Put the pork in the pot, and cover with water. Put on high heat.
Water to cover	
Deep pot with lid	

1 green onion	Crush the green onion and add to the pork. Bring to a boil on high heat, cover and reduce heat to medium low. Simmer until done (about 20 or 30 minutes). Be careful not to overcook.
	Drain off the broth and use for soup or in other recipes. Chill the pork and use as directed in recipes. It can be sliced thin and used as sandwich meat.
	Note that no seasoning, other than the green onion, is used.

BOILED SHRIMP

Buy white shrimp, preferably fresh in the shell. If it is boiled after the shell is removed it will curl and too much of the flavor will be lost. White shrimp has a much gentler flavor than pink or red shrimp, and is especially preferable if the shrimp are not very, very fresh.

Deep pot *2 cups water* *1 green onion*	Crush the green onion and put in the pot with the water. Bring to a boil on high heat. The onion will diminish the strong fishy flavor and odor of the shrimp.
1 lb. (or less) fresh *(frozen) white* *shrimp in the shell*	Put the shrimp into the boiling water, bring to a boil again and boil for only 3 or 4 minutes. Do not defrost frozen shrimp before using them.
	Drain shrimp immediately. Reserve the juice for seasoning or for soup. Cool the shrimp and use as directed in recipes.
	Note that no seasoning, other than the green onion, is used.

BOILED CHICKEN

Use a frying chicken so the meat will be tender and juicy. Use a whole chicken, cut it in half, or use ready-cut pieces.

1 frying chicken *Deep pot with cover* *Water to cover*	Wash the chicken, put in the pot and cover with water. Put on on high heat.
1 green onion *2 slices fresh ginger* *root (optional)*	Crush the onion and add, with the fresh ginger root, to the pot. These two things will counteract the odor of the chicken.
	Bring to a boil on high heat, then reduce the heat to medium low, cover, and simmer until the chicken is tender (about 20 minutes). Poke with a fork: if pink juice comes out, cook a little longer. Be careful not to overcook or it will lose too much flavor.
	Drain off the broth and save for soup. Take the chicken off the bones and use as directed in recipes.
	Note that no salt or seasoning other than the onion and ginger is used.

SHRIMP PASTE

This is the basic element for several recipes. It is made in a mortar of heavy marble, stone or wood (page 9), and is pounded with a pestle of heavy wood or of stone. A small size mortar is useful, but makes it difficult to mix the entire recipe at one time. It is important to follow the steps exactly as given, in order that the flavor will be the best.

1 lb. fresh (frozen) white shrimp
2 cups cold water
1 tsp. borax

Dissolve the borax in water in a bowl. Shell and devein the shrimp and put into the bowl of water, mix well with the hands and let stand about 5 minutes. This cleans the shrimp, calms the fishy odor, and makes the meat firmer. Remove shrimp to a colander and rinse very very thoroughly under running cold water, squeezing with the hands, for about three minutes. The shrimp should be rinsed until it is no longer slippery to the touch. Then squeeze the shrimp with the hands until it is no longer drippy.

Mortar and pestle

Place shrimp in the mortar and begin to pound with the pestle. Pound until the shrimp begins to get soft and pulpy.

1 heaping tbsp. fresh pork fat (or 2 tbsp. cooking oil)

Fat trimmed from pork chops, pork roast, etc., may be used. Chill the fat, so it will be easy to slice. Cut into small pieces. Add to the shrimp in the mortar and continue to pound until it is mixed in.

1 lump (½-tsp. size) rock sugar

Put the lump of rock sugar in the mortar with the shrimp and pound and crush until it is thoroughly mixed. Do not substitute regular sugar—it is too sweet. If rock sugar is not available (try the druggist), omit.

1 shallot (or white part of green onion)

Remove outer skin and slice in very thin rounds. Add to the mixture in the mortar and pound well.

1 heaping tbsp. fresh pork fat (or 2 tbsp. cooking oil)

Chill and slice this second tbsp. of pork fat. Add to the paste in the mortar and pound well.

1 egg white

Put egg white into mortar with paste and mix in well. Keep the yolk for use elsewhere.

1 tbsp. fish sauce

Mix into the shrimp paste in the mortar, a small amount at a time.

Dash of black pepper

Sprinkle on top of the mixture in the mortar and mix in well.

This is the basic shrimp paste recipe called for in several recipes in this book, which appear on pages 32, 105, and 106.

FISH PASTE

This is the basic ingredient for several recipes found in this cookbook. It shows up in soup, steamed, fried, and spread on bread. The fish must be a white fish, with very soft meat. Ladyfish is considered very good for this purpose, but perch or bass may also be used.

2 lb. ladyfish (substitute: perch or bass)	Split the fish open from head to tail. With a spoon or a knife, scrape the meat from the bones and skin. Scrape lightly, gently, a small area at a time. Take your time. It should make a soft, paste-like mass. *Note:* If using bass or perch, it will be necessary to chop or grind the meat after it is removed from the bones and skin. Place in a mixing bowl.
3 tbsp. fish sauce 3 tbsp. water 1 tbsp. cornstarch ¼ tsp. salt ¼ tsp. black pepper	Mix the fish sauce, water, cornstarch, salt and black pepper together until smooth. Add to the fish paste, a small amount at a time, kneading it in with the hands. Knead and mix well, picking out any stray bones or pieces of skin. Wet your hands occasionally with cold water so the fish paste won't stick. *Note:* If you use bass, add another tbsp. of cornstarch.
1 egg white	Reserve the egg yolk for later use in one of the variations on this recipe, or in other recipes. Mix the egg white into the fish paste, squeezing and kneading with the hands, until the paste begins to stick together and form a smooth ball.
1 tbsp. cooking oil	Add a small amount of cooking oil at a time and knead it into the paste thoroughly.
2 medium shallots (or white part of green onion)	Slice the shallots in thin rounds and add to the paste, kneading and mixing well. The paste should have become quite firm, like dough.
3 tbsp. pork fat (substitute: 4 tbsp. cooking oil)	Chill the pork fat, so it will be easier to cut. Use the fat trimmings from pork chops, pork roast, etc. Chop the fat coarsely, and add it to the paste. Knead and mix thoroughly. Recipes using this basic paste are to be found on pages 32, 107, and 108.

COCONUT MILK

Coconut milk is one of the main ingredients for curry in Southeast Asia, and is used in many other dishes. The "milk" is not the watery substance that is found in the center of a fresh coconut, which is called "coconut water," or "coconut juice." The milk is made by grating very fresh coconut and squeezing the grated pulp. If you have a blender, you can make a most satisfactory substitute by following the instructions below.

1 medium-size fresh coconut	Open the coconut by hitting it "between the eyes" on a fine, but visible line that runs around the coconut. Take out the meat, and peel off the brown portion. Slice in fairly fine pieces, and put into the blender. Try using a screwdriver to remove the meat: don't use a knife with a sharp point for it might break off.
2 cups warm water	Add warm water, and turn the blender on low speed for 1 minute. Then turn on high speed for 2 or 3 minutes. Strain through a cloth, twisting the cloth to squeeze all the milk out. Store in refrigerator, and use in recipes as directed. Stir before using. It will keep in the refrigerator about a week or ten days.

NUOC LEO SAUCE

This unusual sauce is used as a dip for several different types of Vietnamese foods. It is very good with BARBECUED PORK (page 42), and with the SALAD "SANDWICHES" (page 96). If you don't live in a large city, you may have to order the Chinese bean sauce, but it is worth the trouble.

½ cup glutinous rice 3 cups water Heavy pot	Put the glutinous rice into a heavy pot with the water, bring to a boil on high heat then reduce the heat to low. Cook, uncovered, until the water is all gone. Stir occasionally. Set aside.
Medium size heavy skillet 2 tbsp. cooking oil 3 cloves garlic ½ lb. ground pork	Crush the garlic thoroughly. Preheat the oil on high heat, then drop in the garlic. When the garlic gives out its odor, add the ground pork and reduce the heat to medium. Saute about 2 or 3 minutes, stirring occasionally.
8-oz. can Chinese bean sauce (page 12)	Add the Chinese bean sauce, stir well, until smooth. Cook another minute.
1 can (1½ cups) chicken broth 3 tbsp. sugar	Add the chicken broth and sugar and stir well. Continue to cook for another minute. Broth from COOKED SHRIMP or BOILED PORK, pages 24 and 23, may be substituted for the chicken broth. Add the cooked rice and continue to cook on medium heat another 5 minutes.
1 cup roasted peanuts (not salted ones)	Crush the peanuts coarsely and add, including all the "dust." Stir well and continue to cook another 5 minutes.
	If the sauce is too thick (experience will tell, but it should be about the consistency of oatmeal or other cooked cereal), add more chicken broth. It can be frozen, in large or small quantities. If frozen, thaw and heat before serving. Serve warm or cold.

CARAMELIZED SUGAR

This is a basic ingredient for numerous Vietnamese recipes, though used in very small quantity. You may find yourself reaching for it to use in other recipes, too, once you have tried it. For instance, as a topping for ice cream, vanilla pudding, or egg custard.

2 tbsp. brown sugar Small sauce pan 1 tsp. water	Heat the brown sugar on low heat with 1 tsp. water until it dissolves and becomes like caramel. It will change to a much darker brown. Stir and shake pan occasionally.
3 tbsp. water	Add this additional water, stir until boiling, and remove from heat. Pour into jar or other container that can be tightly closed for storage. Can be stored in the refrigerator, if desired.

ONION OIL

This onion-flavored oil is used as a garnish in many Vietnamese recipes. It is quick and easy to make, and you will probably find many other uses for it. The flavor is much more delicate than that of green onions sauteed in oil.

Medium-sized skillet
3 tbsp. cooking oil
2 or 3 green onions
Heat-resistant bowl

Chop the green onions, tops and all, and place in a heat resistant bowl. Heat the cooking oil until hot, but not smoking, and pour over the onions. This gives quite a different flavor from fried onions.

Leftover onion oil can be reserved for later use. The oil will keep for several days.

SOUPS

SOUP IS ONE OF THE BASIC ITEMS of a Vietnamese meal, and is often the complete meal. There is an infinite number of soups that can be made by various combinations of the ingredients found in the sample recipes given here. Other soups may be found in the chapters dealing with main dishes, usually with SOUP-SALAD in the title.

In Vietnam, soup is usually eaten over rice, along with the rest of the meal. It is used for the liquid in place of drinking water or tea. Tea is normally served toward the end of or after the meal is finished.

Most soups are served with a side dish of fish sauce (page 15) for individual seasoning to taste. If the soup is not salty enough, more fish sauce is added rather than salt. Chinese parsley and wedges of lemon or lime are also often served as garnish for soup.

PORK AND BEAN CURD SOUP
Four servings

This is a hearty soup, and is a good simple meal served with rice and a salad. It may also be served as an accompaniment to a larger meal. In a restaurant, this recipe might have another six cups of water added and be soup for ten.

2 tbsp. tiny dried shrimp Cold water to cover	Place shrimp in small bowl and cover with cold water. Let soak for ten minutes, or more if convenient. (Optional: substitute a dash of monosodium glutamate, if desired.)
½ block bean curd (about 3 by 3 by 6 inches) 1 tbsp. cooking oil Medium-sized skillet	Cut the block of bean curd in half lengthwise. Blot it dry with a paper towel, squeezing lightly between the hands. This keeps it from popping when it is fried. Heat the oil in a medium skillet, on medium heat. Fry bean curd on its two widest sides, about 2 minutes on each side, using medium heat. This makes it firm. Cut crosswise into ¼-inch pieces, about 1 × 3 inches.
4 quart pot 1 tbsp. cooking oil 1 green onion ½ lb. ground pork ½ tsp. salt	Cut green onion in ¼-inch pieces. Mix half of it with the pork and salt, reserving other half for next step. Heat the oil in the pot. Using medium heat, saute the onion, salt, and pork until pork changes color (about 3 minutes), stirring constantly.
2 large tomatoes	Chop tomatoes coarsely. Add to pork mixture and continue to saute for about one minute or less. Stir occasionally.
	Add the soaked dried shrimp. Saute another minute or less.

3 cups water	Add water to the pork mixture and continue to cook on medium heat until it boils.
	Add the sliced bean curd, and bring to a simmer.
1 tbsp. fish sauce	Add the fish sauce and bring just to a boil.
1 egg	Stir egg just until mixed. Pour into soup and stir several times, using a circular motion in the same direction. This makes strings of cooked egg in the soup. Let the soup simmer 1 or 2 minutes. Don't let it boil after the egg is added.
About 20 chives (optional)	Cut chives in 2-inch sections and add. Remove soup from heat immediately.
TO SERVE	Serve hot. (Can be reheated, but is best served immediately after cooking.) This can be used as a simple soup, but is usually served over rice with a side dish of plain fish sauce to be added to the individual's taste. Leaf lettuce or other salad is an excellent accompaniment.

LOTUS ROOT AND SHORTRIB SOUP　　　　*Four servings*

This subtly-flavored soup is appealing in flavor, and interesting to look at. The lotus root with its many holes looks like round, gray Swiss cheese! The flavor is something like potato, but it is crisp and crunchy.

1½ lb. lotus root	Scrape as you would a carrot. Slice in thin rounds, about ¼ inch thick.
1 lb. pork shortribs (lean) *2 shallots (or white part of green onion)*	Cut shortribs into small serving pieces. Slice shallots in thin rounds.
Soup pot with cover *5 cups water* *¼ tsp. salt*	Put water, shallot, salt, shortribs, and lotus root in soup pot. Bring to a boil on high heat, reduce the heat to medium low, cover, and simmer for 2 hours. There should still be about 2 cups of liquid remaining in the pot.
1 tbsp. fish sauce	Add fish sauce, stir well, and taste. Add more fish sauce if not salty enough. Remove from heat.
TO SERVE	Serve hot, with rice. May be reheated several times.

SHORTRIBS WITH WINTER MELON SOUP　　　　*Six servings*

2 lb. Chinese winter melon (substitute: butternut squash, page 20)	Peel the winter melon, and cut away the soft, pithy center portion with the seeds. Discard peel and center. Cut the firm white section of the melon into strips about 2 inches wide, the length of the piece of melon. Then cut the strips into small strips across, making pieces that are large bite size.

30

1 lb. shortribs (lean)	Cut shortribs into small serving pieces. Slice the shallots into
2 shallots (or white part of green onion)	thin rounds. Put water, salt, shallots, and shortribs into the soup pot. Bring to a boil over high heat. Reduce the heat to
5 cups water	medium high and cook for one hour. There should be about 2
1/4 tsp. salt	cups of liquid remaining in the pot.
Soup pot with cover	

Add the winter melon, bring to a boil and remove from heat after just a few seconds. It just needs to get hot at which point it is cooked enough. If butternut squash is used, cook about 2 or 3 minutes, to taste.

Dash of black pepper — Sprinkle with black pepper before serving.

TO SERVE — Serve hot, with rice if desired.

SHORTRIBS WITH MUSTARD CABBAGE OR GREENS *Four servings*

1 lb. shortribs (lean)	Cut shortribs into small serving pieces. Slice the shallots into
2 shallots (or white part of green onion)	thin rounds. Put water, salt, shallots, and shortribs into the soup pot, bring to a boil on high heat. Reduce the heat to
5 cups water	medium high, cover, and simmer for about an hour. There
1/4 tsp. salt	should be about two cups of liquid remaining in the pot.
Soup pot with cover	

About 1 lb. mustard cabbage (substitute: Chinese cabbage, regular head cabbage or turnip greens)

1 tbsp. fish sauce (or to taste)

Wash the greens, and discard bad spots. Cut the leaf portion into pieces about 2 inches long. Cut the stems into 1-inch pieces. Keep stems and leaves separate. Add the stems to the soup pot, and continue to cook on medium high heat about 2 minutes. Add the fish sauce and stir. Then add the leafy portion, stir well and cook another 2 or 3 minutes. Remove from heat. The leaves will be wilted, but not soft. If not salty enough add more fish sauce.

Dash of black pepper — Sprinkle with black pepper before serving.

TO SERVE — Serve hot with rice. Can be reheated, but the mustard leaves will get soft and the flavor will be changed.

SHORTRIB AND TURNIP SOUP *Four servings*

1 lb. shortribs (lean)	Cut shortribs into small serving pieces. Slice the shallots into
2 shallots (or white part of green onion)	thin rounds. Put water, salt, shallots, and shortribs into the soup pot. Bring to a boil over high heat. Reduce the heat to
5 cups water	medium high and cook for one hour. There should be about 2
1/4 tsp. salt	cups of liquid remaining in the pot.
Soup pot with cover	

1 lb. white turnip — Peel turnip(s) and cut into strips about 2 or 3 inches long and 1/2 to 3/4 inch square. They should be slightly uneven, but almost the same size.

1 tbsp. fish sauce (or to taste)	Add the turnips and the fish sauce to the soup pot, bring to a boil and cook on medium high heat about 5 minutes. If cooked too long the turnips will begin to smell excessively. Remove from heat. Taste. Add more fish sauce if not salty enough.
Dash of black pepper	Sprinkle with black pepper before serving.
TO SERVE	Serve hot, with rice if desired. This can be reheated, but heat quickly and remove from heat before the turnip begins to smell.

FISH CAKE AND CHINESE CABBAGE SOUP *Four servings*

Soup made with the FISH PASTE (page 25) or SHRIMP PASTE (page 25) can be made in various ways, a few of which are described in the following recipes.

1 head Chinese cabbage	Wash the cabbage, and chop the leaves into large pieces (about 3 x 4 inches). Put aside for last step of recipe.
Soup pot with cover *3 cups water* *1 tbsp. fish sauce* *¼ tsp. salt*	Bring the water to a boil over high heat, in the soup pot, then add the fish sauce and salt.
1 cup Fish Paste (page 25) *Cold water in a cup*	Drop the fish paste into the boiling water one teaspoonful at a time, rinsing the teaspoon in cold water between "drops." The fish balls will turn white and float.
	As soon as the fish balls are floating, add the pieces of Chinese cabbage and cover the pot. Let it continue to boil, on high heat, for about 1 minute or until the leaves are just wilted. Remove cover, stir, cover again and continue to cook on high heat another 3 minutes. Turn off the heat and leave the soup covered in a warm place until ready to serve.
TO SERVE	Serve hot. Serve plain, or over rice for a heartier soup. Can be reheated, but do not overcook. Be sure there is a side dish of fish sauce, in case the soup isn't salty enough for individual taste.

FISH CAKE AND WATERCRESS SOUP *Four servings*

A nice, light soup that is still hearty enough for happy eating on a cool day.

1 bunch watercress	Wash watercress thoroughly and remove the coarse stems. Chop into pieces about 2 inches long.
	Substitute the watercress for the Chinese cabbage and continue according to the preceding recipe.

SHRIMP CAKE AND CHINESE CABBAGE SOUP *Four servings*

Here is another recipe for soup having several variations. This one uses SHRIMP PASTE, page 25.

1 head Chinese *cabbage*	Wash cabbage and chop leaves into large pieces, about 3 or 4 inches square. Reserve for last step below.
Soup pot with cover *3 cups water* *1 tbsp. fish sauce* *¼ tsp. salt*	Bring water to a boil in the soup pot, on high heat, and add the fish sauce and salt.
1 cup Shrimp Paste *(page 25)* *Cold water in a cup*	Drop the shrimp paste into the boiling water one teaspoonful at a time, rinsing the teaspoon in cold water between "drops." The shrimp balls will turn white and float.
	Add the Chinese cabbage leaves and cover the pot. Let the soup continue to boil, on high heat, for about 1 minute or just until the cabbage leaves are wilted. Remove cover, stir, cover again and cook for another 3 minutes on high heat. Turn off heat and leave the soup in a warm place, covered, until ready to serve.
TO SERVE	Serve hot over rice, or plain, as a simple soup. Can be reheated before serving, but be careful not to overcook.

SHRIMP CAKE AND WATERCRESS SOUP   *Four servings*

1 bunch watercress	Wash the watercress thoroughly and remove the coarse stems. Chop leaves and tender stems into pieces about 2 inches long and substitute for the Chinese cabbage in the preceding recipe.

SHRIMP BALLS AND BEAN THREAD SOUP   *Four servings*

4-oz. pkg. bean thread *Warm water to cover*	Soak the bean thread in warm water to cover for about 10 minutes, or until soft. When soft enough to cut, chop into pieces about 2 or 3 inches long, using scissors or a sharp knife.
	Substitute the bean thread for the Chinese cabbage in recipe on page 32·

CRAB AND "WESTERN BAMBOO" SOUP   *Four servings*

Asparagus is called "western bamboo" in Vietnam. This soup is quick to prepare, but very hearty and filling. It is especially good on a cool day.

Soup pot
1 tbsp. cooking oil
2 shallots (or white
  part of green onion)
3 or 4 oz. crab meat
  (fresh or canned)
	Slice the shallots in thin rounds. Flake the crab meat. Heat the oil in the cooking pot, and saute the crab meat and shallots on high heat for 1 minute, stirring constantly.

1-lb. can asparagus *spears*	Add the asparagus and stir briskly about 1 minute, shredding the asparagus.

1 can chicken broth (1½ cups) 1 cup water	Add chicken broth and water, stir well, bring to a boil and cook on high heat about 2 minutes.
1 tbsp. cornstarch	Mix the cornstarch with some of the hot liquid in a cup or small bowl until smooth. This keeps it from getting lumpy. Add to the soup and stir well. Bring to a boil, and cook a minute or two until slightly thickened.
1 egg	Stir the egg slightly to mix the white and yolk, then dump it into the soup. Stir immediately, with a circular movement around and around the pot. This makes strings of cooked egg in the soup.
Dash of black pepper	Sprinkle the pepper over the top of the soup, stir, and remove from heat.
TO SERVE	Serve hot, with large slices of lemon or lime for each individual serving, and with black pepper so that each person may season the soup to taste. This soup can be made in advance and reheated.

CRAB SOUP WITH LILY FLOWERS & BEAN THREAD   *Four servings*

This soup is light enough to be served as an accompaniment to a regular meal, but is nourishing enough to be served with a green salad, as a luncheon.

4-oz. pkg. bean thread Hot water to cover	Soak the bean thread in hot water about 10 minutes to soften it. When soft enough, cut it into 3 to 5 inch lengths with scissors or a sharp knife.
½ cup dried lily flowers (optional) Warm water to cover	Soak the dried lily flowers about 10 minutes, or until soft. Break off about ¼-inch of the tough or hard stem end (not the flower end) and discard. Tie each stem in a knot in the middle to make it have a sort of crunch when eaten. Leave the flowers in water until ready to use. If not available, just omit this ingredient.
¼ lb. fresh (frozen) crab meat 1 shallot (or white part of green onion)	Clean crab meat and separate into bite-size chunks. Slice the shallot in very thin rounds.
Heavy soup pot 1 tbsp. cooking oil ¼ tsp. salt Dash of black pepper	Heat the oil in the soup pot, on high heat. Put in the crab meat, shallot, salt and pepper. Saute over high heat, stirring constantly, about 2 minutes.
	Add the soaked lily flowers and stir in.
3 cups water (or chicken stock) 2 tbsp. fish sauce	Add the water (or chicken stock, if a heartier soup is desired) and the fish sauce, and bring to a boil over high heat. Reduce heat to medium and cook for about 5 minutes.
	Add the soaked bean thread and continue to cook over medium heat another 5 minutes.
Dash of monosodium glutamate	Add the monosodium glutamate, stir well, and remove from heat.

TO SERVE	Serve hot, with rice if desired. Should be served with a side dish of plain fish sauce to be added to individual taste, if the soup is not salty enough. Can be reheated.

BEEF AND PINEAPPLE SOUP   *Four servings*

Wait, now! Not sweet, canned pineapple but fresh or unsweetened pineapple. It makes a wonderful vegetable!

½ lb. beef (sirloin or chuck blade roast) *2 green onions*	Slice the beef thin (¼ inch) in pieces about ¾ inch wide and 2 or 3 inches long. Chop the onions fine and mix with the beef.
¼ fresh pineapple *substitute: small can* *of dietary or other* *unsweetened pineapple)*	Chop the fresh pineapple in small chunks, then squeeze it firmly between the hands to get out most of the juice. It will break up into small pieces, much like crushed pineapple. If canned pineapple is substituted, drain well then press as much juice out as possible. Be sure not to use sweetened pineapple.
1 tbsp. cooking oil *Large heavy skillet*	Heat the oil in the skillet and saute the beef and onion about 1 minute, or until beef begins to change color. It should still be pinkish. Remove from skillet and set aside.
4-qt. pot *4 cups water* *1 tsp. salt* *2 tbsp. fish sauce* *1 onion* *Dash of monosodium* *glutamate* *Dash of black pepper*	Cut the onion in 8 or 10 sections and separate. Put the water, salt, fish sauce, onion, monosodium glutamate and pepper in the pot with the crushed pineapple. Bring to a boil on high heat. Turn off the heat and add the beef. (This keeps the beef from getting tough.) Stir and serve immediately.
TO SERVE	Serve hot as a course in a regular dinner, or with rice as a light meal. Can be reheated, but the beef will probably get tough because overcooking toughens it.

SHRIMP AND PINEAPPLE SOUP

Similar to "Beef and Pineapple Soup," this one calls for fresh or unsweetened pineapple, and not the sweet canned type. It makes a delicious vegetable soup.

½ lb. white shrimp *2 green onions*	Shuck the shrimp, wash it well, and chop coarsely. Chop the onions fine and mix with the shrimp.
¼ fresh pineapple *(substitute: small* *can of dietary or* *other unsweetened* *pineapple)*	Chop the fresh pineapple into small chunks, then squeeze it firmly between the hands to get out most of the juice. It will break up into small pieces, much like crushed pineapple. If canned pineapple is substituted, drain well then press as much juice out as possible. Be sure not to use sweetened pineapple.

35

2 tbsp. fat or cooking oil	Heat the fat in the pot. Saute the shrimp and onions for about one minute. Add water, salt, fish sauce, monosodium
4-qt. pot	glutamate, pepper, and crushed pineapple, then bring to a boil
3 cups water	and cook for 2 minutes. Remove from heat and serve.
1 tsp. salt	
2 tbsp. fish sauce	
Dash of monosodium glutamate	
Dash of black pepper	
TO SERVE	Serve hot as a soup accompanying a regular dinner, or with rice as a light meal. It is especially good with "Shrimp Sauce" (page 20). Can be reheated.

BEEF AND TOMATO SOUP   *Four servings*

This hearty soup has an especially nice flavor; it may be served as a light meal with rice, or may be used as a dinner soup, with less beef if desired. It is quickly prepared, taking less than five minutes total cooking time.

1 lb. bottom sirloin	Slice the sirloin against the grain into thin pieces about ¼ inch
3 shallots (or white part of green onions)	thick, 1 inch wide and 2 or 3 inches long. Slice the shallots into thin rounds. Mix the shallots, salt, pepper, and meat together,
½ tsp. salt	and set aside to marinate, or season, for about 30 minutes, if
Dash of pepper	you have time.
2 large tomatoes	Cut the tomatoes in eighths. Remove the seeds if desired.
Large soup pot	Heat the cooking oil in the soup pot. Saute the meat and shallot
1 tbsp. cooking oil	mixture, stirring constantly, on high heat just until the meat begins to turn grey in places (about 1 minute). It should still be pink, or it will get tough. Remove from the pot immediately and reserve.
1 tbsp. cooking oil	Slice the shallot in thin rounds. Heat the cooking oil in the soup
1 shallot (or white part of green onion)	pot, and saute the shallot for a few seconds on high heat, stirring. Add the tomato and continue to saute, stirring, about 1 minute.
3 cups water	Add the water, fish sauce, and salt. Bring to a rolling boil, add
1 tbsp. fish sauce	the beef and remove from heat. Be careful not to overcook or
½ tsp. salt	the beef will get tough. Serve immediately. If not to be served at once, wait until ready to serve to add the meat.
TO SERVE	Serve hot, either plain or over rice. Can be reheated, but the meat will get tough. If leftovers look likely, serve all the meat the first time and have only the soup left over.

GIBLET AND BEAN THREAD SOUP   *Four servings*

Here's an excellent way to use leftover chicken giblets.

1 4-oz. pkg. bean thread	Soak the bean thread in warm water to cover at least 10 minutes. Drain well, and chop coarsely. Set aside.
Water to cover	

½ lb. giblets (frying chicken gizzards and hearts)	Chop the chicken hearts and gizzards into thumbnail size chunks. Slice the shallots in thin rounds. Mix the giblets, with the shallots, salt, fish sauce and pepper, and set aside to season, or marinate, for 20 or 30 minutes.

½ lb. giblets (frying chicken gizzards and hearts)
2 shallots (or white part of green onions)
1 tsp. salt
1 tbsp. fish sauce
Dash of pepper

Chop the chicken hearts and gizzards into thumbnail size chunks. Slice the shallots in thin rounds. Mix the giblets, with the shallots, salt, fish sauce and pepper, and set aside to season, or marinate, for 20 or 30 minutes.

1 tbsp. cooking oil
2 qt. heavy pot

Heat the cooking oil in a deep pot, and put in the seasoned chicken giblets. Saute on medium heat about 3 minutes, stirring occasionally.

1½ cups chicken broth
1½ cups water

Add the chicken broth and water to the giblet mixture in the pot. Bring to a boil, on medium high heat, and boil for about 5 minutes. Add the bean thread and cook for another 3 minutes or so.

TO SERVE

Serve hot, in soup bowls, with a slice of lime or lemon.

CHICKEN-LONG RICE SOUP   *Four servings*

Deep heavy pot
1 lb. chicken backs
1 lb. frying chicken pieces
6 cups water
4 thin slices fresh ginger root (substitute: green onion tops)

Put the chicken in the deep pot with the water and thin-sliced ginger to help get rid of the slightly disagreeable odor of boiling chicken. Bring to a boil and cook on medium high heat for about 30 minutes.

4-oz. pkg. bean thread (long rice)
Warm water to cover

Soak the bean thread in warm water to cover 10 minutes or or more. Drain well and chop coarsely.

Take out the frying chicken pieces, leaving the backs in the pot. When the frying chicken pieces have cooled, remove the meat from the bones and shred it. Skim off the scum from the top of the soup, and decrease the heat to medium.

2 shallots (or white part of green onions)

Crush the shallots with the flat side of a knife blade and add to the soup in the pot.

2 tbsp. fish sauce
½ tsp. salt
Dash of black pepper

Add the fish sauce, salt and pepper to the soup, and let it continue to simmer another 20 minutes.

Add the soaked bean thread and the shredded chicken and cook for another two minutes. Turn off the heat.

TO SERVE

Can be served over rice, or as a soup with dinner. Be sure to serve with a side dish of plain fish sauce for individual seasoning to taste, if it is not salty enough. Garnish with Chinese parsley.

37

CHICKEN AND WINTER MELON SOUP

Four servings

Meaty bones from a frying chicken (or 1 lb. backs and wings) *1 shallot (or white part of green onion)*	If bones are large, chop into egg-size or smaller pieces with a cleaver. Slice the shallot into thin rounds.
1 tbsp. cooking oil *Heavy soup pot*	Heat the cooking oil in the soup pot and saute the shallot and chicken bones on high heat, stirring, for about 2 minutes.
1 qt. water	Add water, bring to a boil and cook over medium high heat about 15 minutes.
1 tbsp. fish sauce *¼ tsp. salt* *Dash of black pepper*	Add seasoning and stir well. Taste, and add more salt or fish sauce if desired. Reduce heat to medium low and cook another 20 or 30 minutes.
2 lb. Chinese winter melon (substitute: butternut squash)	Peel the winter melon, remove the center portion with the largest seeds and the soft section. Slice into pieces about ¼ inch thick and about 1 inch wide and 2 or 3 inches long. Add to the soup and cook about 2 minutes before serving. Use the Chinese winter melon (sometimes called Chinese squash) if possible to find it. Butternut squash is an acceptable substitute, but a smaller amount may be used, and a slightly longer cooking period may be desired—taste it after 2 minutes, and if it is too hard, cook another minute or so.
TO SERVE	Serve as a broth-type soup, or serve over rice, as desired, with a side dish of fish sauce for individual seasoning.

CHICKEN AND RICE SOUP

Eight servings

This soup is a hearty one, but may be served in small quantities as an accompaniment to a main dish; it is excellent as a one-dish luncheon or dinner.

1 cup rice *4 cups water* *3-quart pot*	Put the rice and water into a pot and bring to a boil on high heat. Reduce the heat to medium low and cook, uncovered, until the rice is very soft and the water has disappeared (about 30 minutes), but do not burn the rice. Stir gently 3 or 4 times.
Soup pot *6 cups water* *1 medium frying chicken*	Cut the frying chicken in half and put into the soup pot with the water. Bring to a boil on high heat. Save the giblets for use in another recipe.
1 shallot (or a green onion)	Smash the bulb portion of the shallot, cut the green top into 2 or 3 inch lengths, and add to the chicken in the pot.
10 thin slices fresh ginger root (optional)	Slice the fresh ginger root thin and add to the chicken. This gets rid of the slightly strong "chicken" taste that boiled chicken sometimes has. If fresh ginger is not available, substitute reconstituted dried whole ginger root.
	Continue cooking on high heat for 30 minutes. Take out the chicken and cool. When cool, remove meat from the bones.
	Put the soft rice into the chicken broth and stir well.

Dash of monosodium glutamate	Add the monosodium glutamate, pepper, salt, and fish sauce and turn off the heat.
Dash of black pepper	
¼ tsp. salt	
2 tbsp. fish sauce	
TO SERVE	Before serving, put in a finely chopped green onion. This is a substitute for a special kind of Vietnamese mint that is not usually available elsewhere. Add half of the boned chicken, in medium-sized shreds or chunks. Reserve the remainder of the chicken for use in other recipes. Serve hot, with a side dish of fish sauce for use if not salty enough for the individual taste. A fat wedge of lemon should be served with each bowl, to be squeezed in to taste.
1 green onion	
Lemon wedges	
Fish sauce	

DUCK SOUP   *Ten servings*

Have you heard the old expression "easy as duck soup"? This is easy, and makes a warming, simple soup.

Bones, bony pieces and some extra fat from a duck (or cut up and cook a whole tough duck this way—just cook it a lot longer)	Use a very large soup pot. Duck is flavorful, and will flavor a big pot of soup. Put the duck in the pot with the water and bring to a boil over high heat. (If it begins to boil over, reduce the heat slightly.) Boil for 20 minutes. (If a tough duck is used, reduce heat to medium and cook until the meat is tender—3 or 4 hours if necessary.) Add more water as it boils away, keeping the level about the same.
Large soup pot	
3 to 5 qts. water	
4 or 5 slices fresh ginger root	Skim the scum off the top of the soup, so it will be transparent. Add the ginger root. Slice the green onions in ½-inch pieces and add, with the salt.
2 green onions	
1 tsp. salt	
1 cup rice	Wash the rice and add to the soup. When cooking is finished the rice will be very soft, and the soup will be slightly thickened by the rice. Reduce the heat to low and cook for another 30 minutes, or until tender. If you, like most Vietnamese families, have leftover cooked rice, use 2 cups of that and add about 15 minutes before the cooking is done.
2 tbsp. fish sauce (or to taste)	Add the fish sauce and pepper just before serving. Stir well. If the soup is not salty enough, add more fish sauce or serve with a bowl of fish sauce so each individual may season the soup to taste.
Dash of black pepper	
TO SERVE	Serve hot, in large deep soup bowls, garnished with Chinese parsley if available. Serve with large slices of lemon, to be squeezed gently into the individual bowls to taste. Can be reheated several times. Don't keep more than 2 or 3 days in the refrigerator—the fat causes it to spoil quickly. Can be frozen and stored for longer periods.
Chinese parsley	
Lemon slices	

Notice that, although lots of fat was put into the soup, it comes out not tasting fat.

PORK MAIN DISHES

PORK IS THE MOST COMMON TYPE OF MEAT used in Vietnam, as in most of the orient. It is used either ground or chopped very fine, or sliced in very thin, bite-size pieces. When cooked as a roast, it is often cut into smaller chunks so that the seasonings may soak in better. Most of the beef recipes may also be used for cooking pork.

Pork fat is also much used in Vietnam; as a result of the wide spread use of pork, it is readily available and is a cheap source of cooking fat. In these recipes, cooking oil has been substituted for pork fat in most cases.

POT ROAST PORK

Every well-equipped refrigerator should have a chunk of this inside for all sorts of emergencies.

3 lb. fresh ham roast 4 cloves garlic 1 tbsp. salt 1 tsp. black pepper	Buy lean meat, all in one piece. Slice the garlic in very thin rounds. With the tip of a sharp-pointed knife, make incisions all around the chunk of roast. As each incision is made, with the knife still in the meat, pry the hole slightly open and insert a slice of garlic. Mix the salt and pepper together and rub the surface of the meat well with the mixture. Pull the roast together into a firm tight roll, and tie it tightly with string.
Roasting pan with cover 1 tbsp. cooking oil	Heat the cooking oil in the roaster and brown the meat on all sides, on medium heat.
1 cup cold tap water	Add the water, bring to a boil and reduce the heat to low. Cover and cook on low heat until tender (about 1 hour). Since the water will not cover the meat, uncover and turn the roast over occasionally.
TO SERVE	This is best served cold. Slice thin and serve with a salad, or with leaf lettuce and mint leaves, or with PICKLED BEAN SPROUTS (page 92). It is also good for making sandwiches with French rolls or French bread.

PORK STEW
Six servings

This can be made in advance and reheated repeatedly. It keeps well in the refrigerator about 1 week, and can be frozen very successfully. Every well-stocked refrigerator should have some.

2 lb. fresh lean ham roast	Cut the ham roast into approximately 3-inch chunks (cubes). There won't be many, but the roast should not be left in one large piece.
1 tsp. salt 1 tbsp. sugar 2 shallots (or white part of green onion) 1 tsp. caramel syrup (page 27) ¼ tsp. black pepper ¼ cup fish sauce	Crush the shallots. Combine with the salt, sugar, caramel syrup, pepper and fish sauce, and pour over the cubes of pork. Let marinate, at room temperature, about 1 hour.
Heavy pot with cover 6 cups water	Bring water to a boil in the heavy pot. Put all of the ham and the marinade sauce into the boiling water and bring to a boil again. Skim off the scum, reduce the heat to medium low, cover, and let simmer until tender (about 3 hours). Use the chopstick test: If the end of a chopstick can be pushed into the meat, it is tender.
TO SERVE	Serve hot, with rice, salad, PICKLED BEAN SPROUTS, (page 92) etc. You will probably find many other ways of your own to serve this.

SWEET-SOUR SHORTRIBS   *Four servings*

Quite different from the usual type, and sure to be popular. Fresh pineapple makes both the "sweet" and the "sour" in this recipe.

Large skillet 1½ lb. shortribs 4 cups water 2 shallots (or white part of green onions) 1 tsp. salt	Slice shallots in thin rounds. Cut lean shortribs into serving pieces. Place in large skillet and add shallots, salt, and water. Bring to a boil on high heat, cover and reduce heat to medium. Simmer, covered, for 2 hours. If water evaporates before cooking is completed, add about 1 more cup. If all water is not evaporated at the end of 2 hours, bring heat to high, uncover and boil until water is all evaporated.
⅓ fresh pineapple	Clean pineapple, take out core, then cut into small chunks. Squeeze between the hands, getting out as much juice as possible. This will crush the pineapple. Save the juice for drinking, salads, etc.
2 large carrots	Shred the carrots, using a vegetable peeler or large section of grater.
1 large tomato	Cut tomato in eighths.
2 cloves garlic	Crush the garlic and add to meat in skillet, which will begin to saute in its own fat. Turn heat to medium high. When the smell of the garlic begins to be noticeable, put in the pineapple, carrots and tomato. Saute about 1 minute. Stir often.
1 cup water 2 tbsp. fish sauce	Add the water and fish sauce, stir well, cover and steam about 10 minutes, still on medium high heat.
½ tsp. cornstarch	Take some of the juice from the skillet, mix the cornstarch with it so it won't get lumpy, and stir into the mixture in the skillet. Let cook about 1 more minute. Serve.

VARIATION	If fresh pineapple is not available, use a small can of crushed pineapple and add a tablespoon of vinegar to it, or use canned diet (unsweetened) pineapple.
TO SERVE	Serve hot, with rice, soup, and salad.

PORK SHORTRIBS   *Four servings*

Be sure to get shortribs, the country style with lots of lean meat—don't buy the spareribs that are all fat and bone and very "spare" of meat. This is an appetite teaser, makes you want to eat lots of rice.

1 lb. lean pork short-ribs *2 green onions* *¼ tsp. salt*	Sprinkle the salt over the shortribs. Cut the onions in 2-inch lengths, tops and all, and mix with the shortribs. Let stand 20 or 30 minutes to "season."
Medium skillet with cover *1 tbsp. cooking oil*	Heat the oil in the skillet, and saute the ribs and onions over high heat 2 or 3 minutes, or until the pork has mostly changed color and begins to brown, stirring all the time. Cover and cook 1 minute on high heat.
1 tsp. sugar *¼ cup water*	Mix the sugar and water, remove cover and pour over the shortribs and stir well. Cover again and lower the heat to medium high. Cook about 5 minutes, removing the cover to stir occasionally.
1 tbsp. fish sauce	Turn on ventilating fan. Add the fish sauce, cover, and cook 5 more minutes on medium high heat. Don't be put off by the smell of the fish sauce in this recipe—it is different in taste once the cooking is done.
Dash of black pepper	Sprinkle black pepper over the shortribs, stir, and remove from the heat.
TO SERVE	Serve hot, with rice, soup, and salad. This is very good reheated, and can be frozen.

FANCY BARBECUED PORK ON SKEWERS   *Four servings*

This tender delicacy takes a little time to prepare, and also a little muscle power. The lazy ones might want to use ground pork, but that gives quite a different type of barbecue, and cannot be considered a substitute. Be sure you have the right kind of equipment on hand before starting this recipe. For instance, you need skewers that are long enough to reach across your barbecue grill. Or, as an alternative, a light-weight wire grill to keep the balls of pork from falling into the fire.

1½ lb. very lean pork leg (ham), or pork cutlet	Trim any fat off the pork, and get rid of all bone and gristle. Then slice very thin (⅛ inch) and cut in pieces about 1 inch square.

1 tbsp. rice wine, or sherry (or 1 tsp. rum or brandy) *½ tsp. salt* *½ tsp. sugar*	Mix the wine, salt, and sugar with the pork and let it soak at least 30 minutes. This helps to keep the meat moist when it is barbecued.
2 cloves garlic	Crush the garlic fine. Using a mortar and pestle (see page 9 for instructions), pound the seasoned meat together with the crushed garlic until it all is reduced to a paste. Note that it is much easier to pound a small quantity at a time.
1 tbsp. roasted rice (substitute: roasted soy beans) (optional) *1 tsp. fish sauce* *2 tbsp. lard*	Pound the roasted rice (see page 18) (or the roasted soy beans) to a powder. If neither is available, just omit. Add the powder, along with the fish sauce, to the pork paste. Then mix in the lard. Lard, either bought or rendered from slowly cooked pork fat, is better than vegetable shortening because of the flavor, and because it also contributes to the moistness of the barbecued pork.
Long barbecue skewers (or short, individual wooden or bamboo skewers)	Knead the paste well, with the hands, as if it were dough. Then form the paste into slightly elongated balls on the skewers, putting several balls on a long skewer or one ball on a short skewer. Squeeze the meat firmly when making the balls, and squeeze it firmly onto the skewers so it won't slip off or fall apart while cooking.
Charcoal barbecue equipment	Cook the skewered pork balls over a medium charcoal heat for about 15 minutes or more, depending on the size of the balls, the heat, etc., making sure the pork is well done and slightly browned on the outside. Turn occasionally so that all sides cook evenly. For a small group, this would work well on a rotisserie.
TO SERVE *Leaf lettuce* *Chinese parsley (if available)* *Fresh mint leaves* *Nuoc Leo Sauce* *¼ lb. look fun noodles*	Serve on a central plate. Also serve a central plate of leaf lettuce, mint, and Chinese parsley, and a plate with about ¼ pound cooked *look fun* noodles (page 17). These can be put on top of a lettuce leaf "for looks." Serve with individual bowls of Nuoc Leo Sauce (page 27)
TO EAT	This is something to be eaten with the hands. First, take a leaf of lettuce. On top of it put a few strands of cooked noodles and a piece or two of Chinese parsley and mint. Then put a barbecued pork ball in the nest thus formed, wrap the lettuce leaf closely around all, take a firm grip and dip it into the Nuoc Leo Sauce. Each leaf may call for several dips into the sauce, or if you have small leaves you may prefer to divide the meat balls into several bite-size pieces.

DRY PORK STEW

Four servings

This is considered a very healthful food in Vietnam. It is fed to new mothers, along with rice and a boiled vegetable, as the safest possible food for one in such a delicate condition. It is also eaten by non-mothers, fathers, sons, and anyone else who can get near the dish!

Medium small pot	Use lean pork chops, or pork shoulder. Remove the bones, and
1 lb. fairly lean pork	slice the meat against the grain in thin (⅛-inch) strips about 1
2 shallots (or white	inch wide and 2 or 3 inches long. Slice the shallots in thin
part of green onion)	rounds. Put into a small deep pot—a larger pot will not serve
	for this dish, for it must cook at fairly high heat and yet not
	burn. The small pot presents less surface for burning.
¼ tsp. black pepper	Add the seasoning and water to the pork in the pot, put on high
2 tbsp. fish sauce	heat and bring to a boil. Stir well, mix. and cook about 2 min-
¼ tsp. salt	utes. Reduce heat to medium high, and boil for about 20 to 30
1 tbsp. sugar	minutes, stirring occasionally. All the liquid should be ab-
2 tbsp. water	sorbed by the meat, and it will begin to turn a light brown. Be
	careful not to burn it.
TO SERVE	This will be pretty salty, so serve with lots of rice and a soup
	and salad.

SAFFRON EGGPLANT WITH PORK   *Six servings*

An unusual way with eggplant, this. Good for a hearty dinner, or for lunch on a cold day.

1 block bean curd	Cut the block of bean curd in half. Blot with paper toweling,
about 1½ inches	squeezing lightly, to keep from popping in hot oil. Heat the
thick, 6 inches long,	oil in the skillet on medium heat. Saute both sides of both
3 inches wide (op-	blocks about 2 or 3 minutes, to make firmer, using medium
tional) (page 12)	heat. Slice into smaller sections, making about 8 or 12 pieces
2 tbsp. cooking oil	from each of the larger blocks.
Heavy skillet	
2 tbsp. dried shrimp	Soak the small dried shrimp in warm water about 10 minutes,
(optional: substitute	then boil over high heat about 5 minutes. Drain off water and
a dash of monoso-	reserve it for seasoning other foods, if desired.
dium glutamate)	
Warm water to cover	
½ lb. pork leg, about	Slice the pork in small pieces, about ⅛ inch thick and 1 inch
¾ lean and ¼ fat	wide, 2 or 3 inches long. Try to get a little fat in each slice.
2 tbsp. cooking oil	Using the same skillet used to saute the bean curd, heat the
	cooking oil and saute the pork and soaked dried shrimp,
	stirring occasionally, over high heat for about 1 minute.
2 green onions	Slice the green onions, including the green top portion, in
	small pieces. Add to the pork and continue to saute on high
	heat another minute, stirring occasionally.
1 box fresh mushrooms	Cut the largest mushrooms in half, then wash all gently. Add
(about ¼ lb.)	to the pork, reduce the heat to medium and cook 2 minutes,
	stirring gently occasionally.
2 long eggplants, or 1	Wash eggplant and peel, leaving on a few strips of skin for
medium round egg-	color. Cut in thick finger-size pieces.
plant	
½ tsp. saffron (or 1 tsp.	Add salt, saffron and eggplant to top of pork in skillet. Stir
curry powder)	gently. Cook about 1 minute on medium heat.
½ tsp. salt	

44

1 cup water	Add the water slowly. Then place the bean curd over the top. (From here on do not stir, but add things in layers.) Continue to cook on medium heat another 3 minutes.
1 clove garlic	Crush and chop fine, and sprinkle the garlic over the mixture in the skillet. Do not stir.
2 large tomatoes *2 tbsp. fish sauce*	Remove the stem end, and cut the tomatoes in eighths. Add to the top of the mixture in the skillet, then dribble the fish sauce over the top. Do not stir. Continue to cook on medium heat until done (another 15 or 20 minutes). Total cooking time should be about 30 minutes.
TO SERVE	Serve hot, with rice and salad. Be sure to pour some of the juice over the rice, too. Can be reheated, but do not freeze. It is best when freshly prepared, since the bean curd and the eggplant are fragile and will disintegrate or get mushy.

PORK AND COCONUT WATER STEW   *Six to eight servings*

This delightful dish is included because it is so popular in Vietnam, though it will probably not be possible to duplicate it in many places. The basic ingredient is the water of green coconuts, fresh off the tree. There is no substitute.

Heavy pot with cover *2 lb. fresh lean ham* *roast* *4 cups green-coconut* *water (no substitute)* *1 tbsp. salt* *3 shallots (or white* *part of green onions)* *¼ tsp. black pepper* *¼ cup fish sauce*	Cut the fresh ham into 3-inch cubes (or chunks); there won't be many. Crush the shallots. Use the water from very young, green coconuts—the type that is used for drinking. Mix all ingredients together in a heavy pot, and bring to a boil over high heat, uncovered.
	Skim off the scum, cover, and cook slowly over low heat about 3 hours. The color will change to a very dark, translucent brown.
TO SERVE	Serve hot, with rice, salad, soup, or as a main dish. This can be made in advance and reheated several times. It will keep 1 week in the refrigerator and can be frozen.

CARAMELIZED PORK   *Four or more servings*

This takes a long time to cook, but is very easy to do. In Hue, central Vietnam, pork belly is used in this recipe. Belly is very fat and is considered good in a cooler climate. Don't discard the fat portions before tasting—it is surprisingly good and surprisingly digestible!

1 lb. fresh pork leg (ham)	Cut the fresh ham into several chunks about 1½ to 2 inches square.
2-qt. pot *1 tbsp. cooking oil* *1 tsp. salt* *2 green onions* *Dash of pepper* *1 tsp. sugar*	Chop the green onion fine. Heat the oil in the pot, then add the onion and the remaining ingredients, including the pork. Saute, stirring, on medium heat until the meat is brown (about 5 minutes or more).
4 cups water	Add the water and simmer, uncovered, on medium heat for one hour.
1 tbsp. fish sauce	Add the fish sauce and continue to simmer on medium heat 1 more hour. Most of the water will be absorbed by the meat and the remainder will be slightly thick—or caramelized. Be careful not to burn it.
TO SERVE	Serve hot as a main dish, with lots of rice. This has a very long life—it may be frozen, refrigerated, reheated, served as an appetizer, etc., etc.

VIETNAMESE MEAT LOAF   *Four servings*

This meat loaf is made with pork and steamed, and has quite a different flavor and texture from an American meat loaf. It is very quick, and does not heat up the oven. This is the same mixture that is used to stuff CABBAGE ROLLS, page 49.

6 dried mushrooms *Hot water to cover*	Soak the dried mushrooms in hot water until soft and pliable. (at least 20 minutes). Cut off and discard the hard stem portion, and chop the mushrooms coarsely.
½ cup bean thread *Warm water to cover*	Soak the bean thread in warm water to cover at least 10 minutes. Chop coarsely, then measure out ½ cup for use in this recipe. Any remainder may be used in other recipes.
3 shallots (or white part of green onions) *½ medium onion*	Slice the shallots in thin rounds. Chop the onion coarsely.
1 lb. ground pork *1 tbsp. fish sauce* *½ tsp. salt* *Dash of black pepper*	Add the mushrooms, long rice, shallot and onion to the ground pork. It is better to use finely chopped pork, chopped at home with a heavy, very sharp knife, but ground pork from the butcher's is an adequate substitute. Then add the fish sauce, salt, and black pepper and mix together thoroughly with the hands, or with a spoon or fork, if desired.
4 eggs	Break the eggs into the meat mixture and mix in well with the hands, or a spoon or fork.
Flat heat-proof dish *Steamer*	Place the meat loaf in a heatproof dish and put in the top part of the steamer. (See page 10 for instructions.) Put water into bottom of the steamer, put the top section, with the meat loaf, in place, cover and steam over high heat until firm (about 20 minutes). To test, remove the lid, try the loaf with a fork or spoon, gently.

TO SERVE
Nuoc Man Sauce
Leaf lettuce

This is especially good served with leaf lettuce. Wrap a bite-sized portion of the loaf in a leaf of lettuce, dip into the sauce and eat with appropriate noises of appreciation. Can also be served with rice, with bread, or in any way one might serve meat loaf American style.

LONG RICE AND PORK MIX
Four to six servings

26 rolls of ngun si fun noodles, also known as "rice sticks," or py mei fun (page 18)
Warm water to cover
Deep pot

Put the individual tiny bundles of noodles into warm water to cover. As soon as they have softened enough to make it easy, untie the individual bundles and discard the ties. Soak about one hour.

Put the pot of noodles and the soaking water on high heat. Bring just to the boiling point and remove from heat immediately. Drain at once in a colander. These noodles are very fragile and will disintegrate if cooked very much.

1 egg
1 tsp. cooking oil
Large heavy skillet

Beat the egg with a fork just until the white and yellow are thoroughly mixed. Preheat the skillet with the oil in it on medium heat. Reduce the heat to low and pour in the egg, turning and tilting the skillet so that the egg spreads in a thin layer over the skillet bottom. Cook until the egg is dry. Remove from heat, and when cool enough, roll the egg into a roll about 3 inches wide. Slice across into strips about 1/4 inch wide and set aside.

1/2 cup tiny dried shrimp (optional: substitute a dash of mono-sodium glutamate)
Warm water to cover

Soak the dried shrimp in warm water to cover about 15 minutes. Omit if you don't like, or can't get.

1 lb. fresh pork leg (ham) or pork chop
2 green onions

Slice the fresh pork thin (about 1/8 inch) and cut in pieces about 1 inch wide and 2 inches long. Leave on plenty of fat. Chop the green onion fine, top and all.

Large skillet
3 tbsp. cooking oil

Preheat the oil on high heat, and put in the pork and green onion. Reduce heat to medium and saute about 2 minutes, stirring frequently.

Add in the soaked dried shrimp and stir well (optional).

2 tbsp. salt
Dash of black pepper

Add the salt and pepper and continue to cook on medium heat another 2 minutes, stirring occasionally.

Add in the drained noodles and continue to cook another minute, stirring very gently occasionally.

1 lb. fresh bean sprouts

Add the bean sprouts, mix gently, and continue to cook on medium heat for 2 more minutes. Lift with a spatula from the bottom occasionally to keep from sticking too much.

About 1 cup (loose pack) chives	Cut the chives in 2 or 3 inch lengths before measuring. Add to the mixture in the skillet and mix in gently. Continue to cook on medium heat 2 more minutes, lifting from the bottom with spatula occasionally.
¼ cup water 2 tbsp. fish sauce	Mix the water and fish sauce together, then pour over the noodle mixture gradually, stirring gently to mix in well.
	Add the sliced, cooked egg, mix in gently and remove from heat.
TO SERVE Nuoc Mam Sauce	Serve hot, with side dishes of NUOC MAM SAUCE (page 23). This can be reheated by wrapping in aluminum foil and steaming in a steamer, but if it is stirred too much the noodles will fall apart into tiny bits more like rice.

TROTTING BAMBOO STEW   *Four to eight servings*

This is one of the many ways the Vietnamese prepare pig's trotters—considered a very tasty part of the pig. In Vietnam, fresh bamboo shoots are available during most of the year and they are often used in preparing this dish, but canned bamboo may be substituted. Dried bamboo shoots are used during the rainy season, but the dried bamboo is sun dried for family use and is not intended for storage beyond the three months or so of need. Dried bamboo shoots available in Chinese or other oriental stores in other parts of the world are usually machine or kiln dried, and need considerably more soaking and boiling. Other recipes using dried bamboo are listed in the index under "bamboo, dried."

3 to 4 oz. dried bamboo shoots 3 qts. water	Soak the bamboo shoots overnight. Next day drain and rinse well.
Soup pot Water 1 tsp. baking soda	Put the soaked bamboo shoots in a soup pot with water to cover and add baking soda, which helps to make the bamboo shoots more tender. Bring to a boil and cook, uncovered, over medium heat, about 1 hour. Drain and rinse the shoots under cool running water, rubbing firmly between the hands to clean thoroughly. Drain well. Cut each strip in half across, then cut each half into 3 or so lengthwise strips about ½ inch wide and 2 or 3 inches long. Put the strips back in the soup pot.
2½ lbs. pigs feet 1 tsb. salt 1 tbsp. fish sauce 2 green onions Water to cover	Wash the pigs feet, They will be pretty clean clean when they come from the butcher's, so this won't be too great a job. Then cut into 3–inch sections and put in the soup pot with the strips of dried bamboo. Cut the green onions into 2–inch lengths and add, with the salt and fish sauce. Pour in water to cover. Bring to a boil on high heat. Reduce heat to medium, cover and cook 1 or 2 hours, or until everything is tender. The bamboo shoots should have a slightly firm and chewy texture, similar to that of fresh green onions when only slightly cooked. The flavor is quite different, though. NOTE: If canned bamboo is substituted, begin with this step.

TO SERVE	Remove the bones from the pigs feet. Pull the meat into shreds. Put the meat back into the stew and serve hot, with rice and a salad. Can be served over rice, if desired. This can be stored in the refrigerator several days and reheated. Can be frozen for longer storage.

CABBAGE ROLLS   *Six servings*

This Vietnamese version of the truly international cabbage roll is very quick to prepare, yet it is attractive for a company dinner and hearty for a family one-dish dinner.

14 large outside leaves from cabbage *Boiling water*	In a wide pan, or skillet, bring about a quart or more of water to a rolling boil. Remove any broken outer leaves from the cabbage, then take the large leaves off the head carefully. Immerse each leaf in the boiling water and wilt—about 1 minute or less. More than one leaf can be done at once, just be sure the entire leaf is immersed. An alternate method is to immerse the entire head of cabbage in a pot of boiling water for a minute or two, then remove the outer leaves. The stem section of the cabbage leaves may still be too hard to roll easily. In such a case, with a very sharp knife, pare away a portion of the stem at the back, just making it thinner. Don't cut it away completely.
7 or 8 green onion stems	Use just the green stem portion from little green onions, choosing stems that are at least 8 inches long. The longer the better. These, too, should be wilted in the boiling water for a minute or less, then sliced or torn in half lengthwise. This will provide the ties for the cabbage rolls.
10 dried lily flowers (optional) *6 dried mushrooms* *Hot water to cover*	Soak the dried mushrooms and dried lily flowers (see pages 17 and 16) in hot water until soft and pliable (at least 20 minutes). Remove and discard the stem section of the mushrooms, and pinch off and discard the hard stem end of the lily flowers. Chop all coarsely.
½ cup bean thread *Hot water to cover*	Soak the bean thread in hot water to cover at least 10 minutes. Chop coarsely, using ½ cup for this recipe and reserving any remainder for other recipes.
3 shallots (or white part of green onions) *½ medium onion* *1 lb. ground pork* *1 tbsp. fish sauce* *½ tsp. salt* *Dash of black pepper*	Slice the shallots in thin rounds. Chop the onion coarsely. Mix the chopped lily flowers, mushrooms, bean thread, shallots, and onion with the ground pork. Add fish sauce, salt and pepper, and mix thoroughly with the hands, or with a spoon or fork.
1 egg	Break the egg into the mixture and mix in well. This mixture may also be used for the MEAT LOAF recipe on page 46.
	Place about 2 tbsp. meat mixture near the stem end of a cabbage leaf. Fold the two sides over, then roll lengthwise to

make a roll about 4 inches long. Tie gently with the wilted green onion tops.

2 tbsp. cooking oil Large heavy skillet with cover	Heat the cooking oil in skillet on medium high heat. Place the cabbage rolls in the skillet close together. Cover and cook 2 minutes on medium high heat. Remove the cover and turn the rolls, using tongs, chopsticks, or two spoons and working very gently. Remove from heat if you feel too rushed or awkward. Cover and cook 2 minutes longer.
1 shallot (or white part of green onion) 1 green onion ½ cup tomato sauce ¾ cup water 1 tbsp. fish sauce	Slice shallot and green onion in thin rounds. Make a small space in the middle of the pan, pushing the rolls gently aside. Put in the shallot and green onion and saute a few seconds, until the odor rises. Then pour in the tomato sauce and water. Stir gently around the rolls. Sprinkle fish sauce over the top. Cover and cook for 2 more minutes. Remove cover and turn the rolls again. Cover and cook 6 more minutes. The center of the rolls should be firm when the flat of a spoon is pressed against the top.
1 tsp. cornstarch ¼ cup water Pinch of monosodium glutamate	Mix the cornstarch and monosodium glutamate into the water, which will keep the cornstarch from being lumpy. Pour into the center of the pan, and stir around the rolls gently. This will not make a thick sauce, but it will be thicker than just plain water. Cook 2 more minutes. The total cooking time after the first water is added should be about 10 minutes.
TO SERVE	Serve with rice. Be sure to serve the gravy with the rolls, to pour over the rice. If desired, the rolls can be sliced in half, across the middle. Wait until slightly cooled and it will be easier to slice the rolls without tearing them.
SUGGESTION	If you want to serve fewer people, save out a portion of the meat mixture, add another egg or two to it (depending on how much is reserved—a total of 3 or 4 eggs for the entire recipe), and steam in a small bowl for another meal. See VIETNAMESE MEAT LOAF, page 46.

STUFFED CUCUMBER SLICES   *About six servings*

This is a fancy-looking, elegant-tasting, and easy-to-make dish.

10 dried lily flowers (optional) 5 dried mushrooms Warm water to cover	Soak mushrooms and dried lily flowers in warm water to cover about 15 minutes. Drain; discard tough stem portion of mushrooms and pinch off hard stem end of lily flowers. Chop coarsely.
½ of 2-oz. pkg. bean thread Warm water to cover	Soak bean thread in warm water to cover about 15 minutes. Drain and chop coarsely.
½ lb. fairly lean ground pork 1 green onion 1 tbsp. fish sauce ¼ tsp. salt Dash of pepper	Ask the butcher to grind fresh ham or shoulder, about ¼ fat and ¾ lean. The best, however, is chopped at home with a very sharp knife. Chop the green onion fine and mix with the pork, together with the fish sauce, salt and pepper. Mix in the chopped mushrooms and bean thread. Let the mixture stand to season at room temperature about 20 minutes; if refrigerated, about an hour.

1 egg	Break the egg into the meat mixture and mix in well.
2 large, fat cucumbers	Peel the cucumbers and cut into ¾–inch rounds. Hollow out the center and seeds of each round, leaving just the outer core. Fill in the hole, all the way through, with the meat mixture, rounding it up slightly on both sides and packing firmly.
2 tbsp. cooking oil Heavy skillet	Preheat the oil, and fry the stuffed cucumbers, on medium heat, about 5 minutes on each side, turning occasionally, to brown. Be sure the center is done.
SAUCE 1 clove garlic	Crush the garlic, make a small space and add to the center of the skillet. Fry a few seconds, until the odor rises.
⅓ cup water ¼ tsp. cornstarch Dash of monosodium glutamate	Mix the water, monosodium glutamate and cornstarch, so it won't get lumpy, then pour into the skillet. Stir gently so it will go around the cucumber slices. Cook for a few seconds, then turn the cucumbers over. When the sauce gets translucent, turn off the heat.
SAUCE VARIATION ¼ cup tomato sauce ½ cup water 1 tsp. cornstarch Dash of monosodium glutamate	As a slightly more spicy substitute for the sauce above, mix the tomato sauce, water, monosodium glutamate, and the cornstarch so it won't get lumpy. Pour the mixture into the skillet and stir gently so it will go around the cucumber slices. Cook a few seconds and turn all the cucumbers over. When the sauce thickens slightly, turn off the heat.
TO SERVE	Serve hot, with rice. Can be refrigerated and reheated, but do not try to freeze—the cucumbers will get soggy. This is best served as soon as it is cooked.

STUFFED TOMATO   *Four or five servings*

This may be steamed or fried, and makes an elegantly different party dish.

5 large tomatoes, or 7 smaller ones	Cut out the stem end of the tomatoes and gently scoop out the center portion of the meat and seeds. Set aside.
STUFFING 3 dried mushrooms Water to cover	Soak the mushrooms about 10 minutes in warm water to cover. Drain well. Cut away and discard the stems. Slice and chop the mushrooms into fine pieces.
¼ of a 2-oz. pkg. bean thread Warm water to cover	Soak the bean thread in warm water to cover at least 10 minutes, and drain well. Chop coarsely.
2 shallots (or white part of green onions) ½ lb. ground lean pork ¼ tsp. salt Dash of pepper 1 tbsp. fish sauce	Slice the shallots into thin rounds. Combine with the ground pork. Add the mushrooms, the bean thread, salt, pepper, and fish sauce. Mix together thoroughly.
1 egg	Break the egg into the pork mixture, and mix in well. It is much easier to get all ingredients combined well if the mixing is done with a kneading motion with the hands, much as one would knead dough.
TO STUFF	Stuff the pork mixture into the center of the tomatoes, stuffing firmly but gently and smoothing the top into a heaping mound.

51

TO STEAM *Steamer* *(see page 10)*	Place the stuffed tomatoes, stuffing side up, on a heat-resistant flat dish in the top section of a steamer. Bring water to boil in the bottom of the steamer, set the top in place, cover, and steam over medium high heat until done (about 30 minutes). The pork should be cooked all the way through.
TO FRY *3 tbsp. oil* *Heavy skillet with lid*	Heat the oil in the skillet, on medium heat. Place the stuffed tomatoes, gently, with spatula, large spoon, or hands in the skillet with the stuffing side *down*. Cover lightly—but be sure plenty of air can get in so the tomato skins won't split open too much. Saute on medium high heat about 4 or 5 minutes. Turn the tomatoes, using a spatula and large spoon. Be very gentle and work slowly, to avoid breaking the skin and making everything come apart. Remove from heat, if you prefer. Saute on medium high heat another 2 or 3 minutes. Reduce heat to low and allow to stay warm until done (about 10 to 15 minutes).
TO SERVE	Can be served "Western style" as a main dish, with rice and a salad. The Vietnamese style is to place a tomato in a deep rice bowl, and add rice on top, eating with chopsticks.

NOODLE SALAD-SOUP (MI QUANG) *Four servings*

This delightful dish is a combination of main dish, soup, and salad. It can be cooked and served with many variations, but the end product is always hearty and a real challenge to a weak appetite. The version described in the basic recipe below is a regional dish from South Central Vietnam, south of Hue. Other versions, with beef and chicken, are given on pages 62 and 84.

½ cup tiny dried shrimp *Warm water to cover (optional: substitute ½ tsp. monosodium glutamate)*	Soak the dried shrimp in warm water about 10 minutes or more, until they begin to soften slightly. Drain just before adding to soup.
1 lb. pork belly (or ¾ lb. pork belly and ¼ lb. pork liver) *2 green onions*	Use pork belly for this recipe. It is striped meat, some fat, lean. Cut it into thin (⅛ inch) slices about 2 inches x ½ inch, across the grain, with some fat and some lean in each piece. Chop the green onion in small pieces. If desired, ¼ pound liver may be used for flavor.
2 tbsp. cooking oil *3-qt. pot*	Heat the oil in the pot and saute the pork and onion on medium heat about 5 minutes, stirring occasionally.
1 tsp. salt	Add salt and the soaked and drained dried shrimp, stir well, and cook for another 5 minutes on medium heat, stirring occasionally.
1 tsp. Chinese shrimp sauce (optional) (substitute: pinch of	Mix the Chinese shrimp sauce with the water, and add to the soup. Stir well and cook about 2 more minutes. Since many people dislike the smell, and some also dislike the taste, of the

monosodium glut-amate and ½ tsp. salt)	Chinese shrimp sauce, another ½ tsp. of salt and a pinch of monosodium glutamate may be substituted. The shrimp sauce is quite salty, so the substitution is for that attribute alone—the flavor and odor are simply omitted.
½ cup water	
3 large tomatoes	Cut the tomatoes in sixths and add to the soup; cook another two minutes, stirring occasionally.
2 cups water	Add the water, bring to a boil, then add the fish sauce. Stir well, and cook another minute.
1 tbsp. fish sauce	
Dash of black pepper	Add the black pepper (coarsely ground is better), stir, and remove the soup from the heat. Keep warm until served.
OTHER INGREDI-ENTS	If the fresh noodles are available, use them. If fresh noodles are not available, substitute the dried Chinese rice noodles called *look fun*, or the Chinese "rice sticks" called *sha ho fun*. Be careful about cooking the dried noodles—some brands have misleading English directions on the package! Soak the dried noodles for two hours in warm water to cover. Bring 6 cups of water to a boil, drain the noodles and add to the boiling water. Bring to a boil again, and boil for 5 minutes. Drain immediately, and rinse under running cool water to separate the noodles and keep them from getting sticky. The dried noodles usually come cut in the proper size, but the fresh noodles should be cut into strips about 3 or 4 inches long, and about ½ inch wide. Set aside.
½ lb. fresh or dried rice noodles (Chinese look fun, *page 17)*	
¼ cup fresh bean sprouts	Wash and drain the bean sprouts, lettuce, Chinese parsley, and mint leaves. Slice the cucumber into ⅛-inch rounds, then cut into narrow strips. This is the salad portion of the dish; set aside for later use.
½ cucumber	
6 or 7 lettuce leaves	
½ cup Chinese parsley	
¼ cup fresh mint leaves	
1 oz. pkg. corn chips	This is a substitute for a very similar Vietnamese food item made of rice. Crush the corn chips coarsely, and set aside for later.
½ cup roasted (salted) peanuts	Chop the peanuts coarsely, just before serving. Be sure to use the "dust" in the bottom of the container, too, because much of the nice flavor is there.
3 tbsp. cooking oil	Chop the green onions fine, tops and all. Place in a heat resistant bowl or small pan. Heat the cooking oil, and pour over the chopped onions. Let stand until slightly cool.
2 green onions	
TO SERVE	Gather together all the bowls and pots of ingredients, and combine in the following order: In the bottom of each soup bowl place ¼ of the salad mixture. Over that, put ¼ of the cooked noodles. Then ladle a nice generous helping of soup with lots of meat over the noodles. On top, sprinkle the corn chips and peanuts, and pour 1 tbsp. onion oil over the top of each bowl. Serve with chopsticks, and soup spoons.
4 deep soup bowls	
EATING INSTRUC-TIONS	With chopsticks, mix everything together, but only as much as individual taste dictates. Eat the meat, noodles, salad greens, etc., with chopsticks, and drink the soup with a spoon. If seconds are desired, have some more soup!

PORK SHRIMP AND VEGETABLE PANCAKE-OMELET (Banh Xeo)

This very Vietnamese dish is hard even to name in English! *Banh* is a very general word, meaning any bread, cake, cookie, or pancake type of food. *Xeo* is the noise that the thin batter makes when it is poured into the hot pan. But there are a lot of other ingredients, and the final product is most memorable. *Six servings.*

THE BATTER
1 cup rice flour
2 cups water
½ cup coconut milk (page 26)
1 tbsp. sugar
1 tsp. saffron
½ to 1 cup finely chopped green onion tops

Mix the rice flour, water, and coconut milk to form a basic very thin batter. Stir in the sugar, or use CARAMELIZED SUGAR SYRUP, page 27, to make the cooked pancake crunchy. Add some saffron, to give the batter a tiny touch of color. And finally gently mix in the finely chopped green onion tops for both color and flavor. Especially color. After the first pancake is cooked, if the batter seems too thin add 1 or 2 tbsp. plain flour. If too thick, add a little more water. It should be very, very thin and runny.

½ lb. pork belly
1 medium onion

Slice the pork belly very thin (⅛ inch), in small pieces (1 × 2 inches or less). Slice the onion very thin.

½ lb. dried mungo beans (optional, but with a definite change of flavor if omitted)

This type of dried bean is usually bought already skinless and halved in Vietnam. When found outside Vietnam, though, the beans must be soaked overnight in lots of water to soften them. Then next day, drain and rinse under cool running water, rubbing firmly between the hands to remove the outer skin. Cover the soaked, rinsed beans with water and the loosened skins will float to the top, where they can be poured off. This may have to be repeated several times, to remove as much of the outer skin as possible.

Pot with cover
Water

Put the rinsed beans in a pot, and put enough water in to cover to a depth of two inches. Bring to a boil, on high, and let boil about 1 minute, not more.

Drain off all the water, leaving the beans in the pot. Put the pot of drained beans back on lowest heat and let cook until dry, for about 30 minutes. Then it is ready to use.

12 fresh (frozen) white shrimp

Thaw shrimp, if frozen. Hull shrimp and clean out the black vein along the back. Using a very sharp knife, slice each shrimp into 3 thin lengthwise slices.

MAKING THE OMELET
Heavy skillet
2 tbsp. cooking oil

Preheat the oil on high heat. To make the first pancake: Put in 3 or 4 slices of the pork and 3 or 4 slices of onion. Saute on high heat, stirring constantly, about 1 minute. Add 2 or 3 pieces of shrimp and cook, stirring, for another few seconds.

Pour ½ cup of the batter over the pork, shrimp, and onion. This is when it makes the sound *xeo*.

1 lb. fresh bean sprouts

Drop a handful of fresh bean sprouts over the top of the "pancake" and scatter 2 tbsp. of the soaked and cooked mungo beans over the top.

2 eggs
2 tbsp. water

Mix the eggs together thoroughly, then mix in the water. Dribble 2 tbsp. of this mixture around the outer edge of the pancake. All of the preceding four steps should have been done rapidly. After the pancake has cooked only a few seconds, cover the skillet and let it continue to cook on medium heat about 1 minute. Uncover the skillet, and fold the pancake in half, with a spatula.

Put the pieces of pork and onion for the next pancake in the exposed half of the skillet, adding a small amount of cooking oil if necessary. Continue to cook for another ½ minute.

Remove the first pancake-omelet to a warm plate, and the second one is already under way. Begin with the step where the shrimp is added and continue from there. Repeat until all the ingredients are gone. The first *Banh Xeo* is usually slightly burned and generally not as nice as the others, just as often happens with pancakes.

TO SERVE
Nuoc Mam Sauce
Chinese parsley
Fresh mint leaves
Thin slices of cucumber
Leaf lettuce

Serve hot, with leaf lettuce, fresh mint leaves, Chinese parsley, thin sliced cucumbers, and individual small bowls of Nuoc Mam Sauce (page 23). Each individual may be served a whole pancake, or only a part. To eat, wrap a portion of pancake in a lettuce leaf with mint, Chinese parsley and cucumber, and dip in the sauce.

PORK OMELET
Four servings

This omelet is a colorful, quick and inexpensive dish that makes a good main course for a simple meal. It bears only a passing resemblance to Egg Foo Yung. It is an easy extra dish when leftovers don't stretch quite far enough, or an unexpected guest arrives just at meal time.

1 green onion
1 large tomato

Chop the green onion into ¼-inch pieces. Seed the tomato and chop coarsely. Add half the chopped onion to the tomato and set aside.

½ lb. ground pork
Dash of black pepper
¼ tsp. salt

Add the other half of the chopped green onion to the pork. Add salt and sprinkle with pepper. Mix.

Medium skillet
1 tsp. cooking oil

Heat the oil in skillet, on high heat. Add the pork mixture, reduce the heat to medium, and saute with occasional stirring until the pork changes color. This will take 3 to 5 minutes.

Add the chopped tomato and onion, stir well, and let the mixture continue to cook on medium high heat another 1 to 2 minutes. Remove from heat and let cool a few minutes.

5 to 8 eggs
1 tbsp. fish sauce

The number of eggs to use will depend on the size of the eggs, the size of the appetites, and the size of the meal. Beat the eggs with a fork until thoroughly mixed, but the white should still be ropy. Add the fish sauce, and stir until mixed in.

10-inch iron skillet, or
other heavy skillet,
or omelet pan. (If a
large skillet is not
available, make two
batches in a smaller
skillet.)
1 tsp. cooking oil

Heat the cooking oil on high heat until it smokes. Add the cooked pork mixture to the eggs, and pour all into the slightly smoking skillet. Reduce heat immediately to medium. With a spatula, push through the mixture to the skillet bottom, lifting slightly so that the uncooked liquid portion can run through to the bottom. Continue this poking and lifting all over the bottom of the pan, but gently, while the mixture cooks for about one minute or so. Reduce the heat to low, and let the omelet sit in the skillet undisturbed about 5 minutes. It should be firm, slightly brown on the bottom, but still soft on top. Fold in half with a spatula, soft top sides together, and remove gently to a warm plate.

TO SERVE
Nuoc Mam Sauce
Leaf lettuce
Chinese parsley
Mint leaves

Serve with rice, a salad, and a soup if desired. A side dish of NUOC MAM SAUCE (page 23) should be served as an accompaniment to be used to individual taste. Leaf lettuce, Chinese parsley, and mint leaves are especially good with this.

BEEF MAIN DISHES

BEEF IS NOT WIDELY USED IN VIETNAM, and tender beef is considered quite a delicacy. The best cuts of beef for use in these recipes will be the chuck blade roast (lower part of the chuck, with only the small shoulder blade bone) when it is well marbled with fat; or sirloin steak. If your butcher does not advertise chuck blade roast, ask for it. He will know what you want.

Beef is normally cut in very thin slices, in bite sized pieces, and will be cooked a very, very short time. It is best to leave the beef slightly pink, so that it will be tender, when it is being sauteed. When beef is boiled, it should be put in at the last minute just before the dish is served; tough beef is not considered a delicacy!

BEEF STEW (THIT BO KHO)   *Four servings*

A hearty dish, and so appetizing that weight-watchers should beware. Every time I cook this, we all get fat! But it is worth the price, occasionally.

2 lb. stewing beef
2 fresh citronella roots
  (optional)
2 shallots (or white
  part of green onions)
	Cut the stewing beef into 2-inch cubes. Crush the citronella roots. If citronella is unavailable, substitute 3 knobs of fresh or reconstituted dried ginger root sliced thin. Crush the shallots.

Heavy pot with cover 1 tbsp. cooking oil 1 tbsp. salt 3 pinches of black pepper	Heat the oil in the heavy pot, and put in the beef, crushed citronella, and crushed shallots. Sprinkle with the salt and pepper. Saute over high heat about 2 minutes, stirring constantly.
2 qts. water 1 tbsp. fish sauce 4-inch stick of cinna- mon	Break up the cinnamon and add, with water and fish sauce, to the beef in the pot. Bring to a boil over high heat. Lower the heat to simmer, cover, and cook on low heat until beef is tender (about 2 or 3 hours).
1½ tbsp. tomato paste	About ten minutes before serving, add tomato paste and stir well. Use Spanish-style tomato paste.
TO SERVE	Serve hot, with rice, spaghetti, or noodles. This is also good reheated—if there is any left over. It can also be frozen.

SESAME, BAMBOO, AND BEEF   *Six servings*

Both bamboo and sesame seed are much used in Oriental cookery. This dish, combining the two, is especially good.

½ lb. top sirloin (or other similar beef)	Slice the beef into thin (⅛-inch) pieces, about 1 inch wide and 2 inches long. Slice against the grain, so it will be tender when cooked.
2 tbsp. cooking oil Heavy skillet	Heat the cooking oil in the skillet, on high heat. Add the beef slices and saute until beef just begins to turn gray (about 1 minute). It should still be mostly pink. Remove from skillet and set aside. Overcooking will make the beef tough, and it gets cooked more later in the recipe.
1 large can and 1 small can bamboo shoots (about 2 cups shredded bamboo) 1 shallot (or white part of green onion)	Be sure to use canned Chinese bamboo shoots. Shred the bamboo shoots into matchstick-size pieces. Slice the shallot in thin rounds.
2 tbsp. cooking oil 1 tbsp. fish sauce ¼ tsp. salt	Heat the cooking oil in the same skillet used to saute the beef. Add the shallot and saute, stirring, on medium heat about half a minute. Add the bamboo shoots, salt, and fish sauce and continue to saute on medium heat about 6 minutes, stirring occasionally.
2 small cloves garlic	Crush the garlic and add to the mixture in the skillet. Stir well to mix. Continue to saute on medium high heat another minute, stirring occasionally. Return beef to the skillet.
3 heaping tbsp. crushed sesame seed	Roast the sesame seed (see page 19) and crush slightly with mortar and pestle to bring out all the flavor. They should be roasted and crushed just before using. Add to the bamboo shoots and beef, stir well and cook just a few seconds. Remove from heat immediately.
TO SERVE	Serve hot, with rice and green salad. This can be reheated before serving. Can be refrigerated for several days, and reheated; or frozen for future use.

BEEF AND SQUASH   *Four servings*

In Vietnam the Chinese *see kwa* squash is used in this recipe. Zucchini squash is different in flavor, but a very acceptable substitute. A hearty dish.

½ medium onion 2 green onions 1 lb. (or less) chuck blade roast	Cut the onion into four pieces. Cut the green onions into 2-inch lengths, tops and all. Slice the beef thin (¼-inch) against the grain, so it will be tender, in pieces about 1 by 3 inches.
1 tbsp. cooking oil Large heavy skillet	Heat the oil in the heavy skillet, on high heat. Saute the onion and green onion about half a minute on high heat then add the sliced beef. Saute, stirring, on high heat a minute or less—just until the beef begins to turn gray but is mostly still pink. Remove from the skillet and set aside.
2 large zucchini squash (a substitute for Chinese see kwa)	Peel the squash, leaving on a few narrow strips of skin for color. Cut into slightly larger than finger-size chunks about 2 or 3 inches long. Set aside.
1 2-oz. pkg. (or less) bean thread Warm water to cover	Soak the bean thread in warm water to cover at least 10 minutes. Drain before using, and chop into 4 or 5 inch lengths, using shears or a heavy knife.

1 clove garlic 2 tbsp. cooking oil	Using the same skillet, heat the oil on high heat. Crush the garlic and saute on high heat a few seconds, until the odor rises. Add the zucchini squash and stir. Reduce the heat to medium and cover. Saute about 1 minute, removing the cover to stir several times.
½ cup water ¼ tsp. salt 1 tbsp. fish sauce	Mix the water, salt, and fish sauce together and add to the squash. Stir well, cover and continue to cook on medium heat about 5 minutes. Squash should be tender but not too soft. Add the drained bean thread and stir well.
1 scant tsp. cornstarch ¼ cup water Dash of black pepper	Mix the cornstarch with the water, to keep it from getting lumpy. Add to the squash and stir lightly. Add the sauteed beef, stir, and cook just a few seconds. Remove from heat, so the beef won't get tough and the squash won't get soft.
TO SERVE	Serve hot with rice and a salad. Can be served as an accompaniment to another main dish. This is best served right from the stove. It can be reheated, but the meat might get tough. Not too good frozen—the squash disintegrates and the beef toughens.

BEEF AND BAMBOO SAUTE   *Four servings*

This is amazingly fast to prepare and will disappear almost as fast when it is served.

½ lb. beef sirloin 1 shallot (or white part of green onion)	Slice the beef thin (⅛-inch) against the grain, in pieces about 1 inch wide and 2 or 3 inches long. Slice the shallot in thin rounds.
1 tbsp. cooking oil Large heavy skillet 1 tbsp. fish sauce	Heat the oil in the skillet on high heat. Put in the beef and the the shallot and saute, stirring, about 1 minute. If cooked longer the meat will get tough. The beef will begin to change color but be mostly pink. Remove from skillet, add fish sauce to the beef, stir well, and set aside.
15-oz. can bamboo shoots	Be sure to get Chinese bamboo shoots—the flavor is better for this dish. Slice the bamboo shoots thin (⅛-inch), in pieces 1 or 2 inches wide and 2 or 3 inches long. Because of the shape of the bamboo shoots, the pieces will be quite irregular in shape.
2 tbsp. cooking oil	In the same skillet used to saute the beef, heat the cooking oil on high heat. Add the bamboo shoots and saute on high heat, stirring, about 1 minute.
1 clove garlic ¼ tsp. salt	Crush the clove of garlic, make a space in the center of the skillet and drop it in. Sprinkle the salt over. When the garlic begins to give out with a garlicky smell, after a few seconds, add the beef and stir well.
¼ cup water 1 tsp. cornstarch	Mix the water and cornstarch, and pour into the beef and bamboo mixture. Stir well, cook a few seconds until the juice thickens slightly and remove from heat. Do not overcook—the meat gets tough if cooked too long.
TO SERVE	Serve hot with rice, soup, and salad. This may be reheated, but is best freshly cooked. If frozen, thaw before warming.

BEEF AND GREEN BEAN SAUTE   *Four servings*

This is another quick-and-easy, nutritious dish that is good served as a main dish for a light meal, or as a side dish at a heavier dinner.

2 lb. fresh green beans (substitute: 2 pkg. frozen French-cut green beans)	Wash the green beans and slice each bean in half lengthwise, then into 2 or 3 inch lengths. (If desired, frozen French-cut beans may be used.) The beans will not be as sweet or as crisp, though. If using frozen beans, defrost slightly before using, and add directly to the beef in the skillet, omitting the step following this one.
Large skillet *4 cups water* *1 tsp. salt*	Bring the water and salt to a boil in the skillet and add the fresh beans. Bring to a boil again, remove from heat and drain in a colander immediately. Set aside. Omit this step if using frozen beans.
1 lb. beef sirloin or chuck blade roast *2 shallots (or white part of green onions)*	Slice the beef thin ($\frac{1}{4}$-inch) across the grain in pieces about 2 inches square. Slice the shallots in thin rounds.
2 tbsp. cooking oil	In the same skillet used to blanch the beans, heat the oil. Put in the sliced beef and shallots and saute, stirring constantly, on high heat for about one minute, or until the beef begins to change color but is still partly pink. Do not overcook. Remove from the skillet and set aside.
2 tbsp. cooking oil	Using the same skillet, heat more cooking oil on high heat. Put in the drained beans, reduce the heat to medium and cook about one minute, stirring occasionally.
½ tsp. salt	Add the salt, stir well, and cook one more minute.
1 clove garlic	Crush the garlic well. Make a vacant spot in the middle of the skillet where the beans are cooking and drop in the garlic. Cook a few seconds, or until you can smell the garlic odor, then stir in. Continue to cook 3 minutes, on medium heat, stirring occasionally.
1 tbsp. fish sauce	Add the fish sauce, stir well.
	Add the cooked beef, stir well, and remove from heat. Should be served immediately.
TO SERVE	Serve hot, with rice. Can be reheated, but the beef will get tough and the beans soggy. Reheat by saute method, on high heat, stirring for a minute or so, just until hot.

VIETNAMESE BEEF AND CABBAGE   *Four servings*

This is quite a switch on the corned beef and cabbage familiar to so many in the Western world. It takes only a few minutes to prepare, and the cabbage doesn't have time to get limp, much less begin to smell like cooked cabbage. A good quick dinner, and not expensive to prepare.

½ lb. chuck blade roast	Cut beef in thin (⅛-inch) slices, about 1 inch wide and 2 inches long.
1 shallot (or white part of green onion)	Slice shallot in thin rounds and add to the beef.
Large skillet 1 tbsp. cooking oil	Heat the cooking oil on high heat, then saute the beef and shallot, stirring constantly until the beef begins to change color but is still mostly pink (about one minute). Remove from the skillet and set aside.
1 medium-size head of cabbage	Cut the cabbage in half or fourths, remove the hard part of the stem, then cut fine (or shred) as for cabbage slaw.
1 tbsp. cooking oil	Heat the oil in the same skillet, and saute the cabbage, stirring constantly, on medium heat for 2 minutes.
1 clove garlic	Crush the garlic, chop fine, and stir into the cabbage.
1 or 2 fresh tomatoes	Cut the tomato in sixths. Stir into the cabbage, reduce the heat to medium low, and continue to cook 1 minute.
	Stir in the beef.
1 tbsp. fish sauce ¼ tsp. salt	Add the fish sauce and salt, continue to stir on medium heat about half a minute.
¼ cup water ½ tsp. cornstarch	Mix the water and cornstarch, then stir into the beef and cabbage. This gives a soupy gravy. Turn the heat to high, stir for about half a minute and remove from heat.
TO SERVE	Serve hot, with rice, and a salad. Can be refrigerated and reheated. Leftovers can be frozen, but the meat will not be so tender and the cabbage will be limp. If frozen, thaw before reheating.

NOODLES WITH SLICED BEEF (SAUTE) — *Four servings*

This is a variation of the preceding recipe, and it is another good one-dish meal. It should be served with all ingredients cold except the sauteed beef strips, which should be hot.

1 lb. chuck blade roast	Trim off the excess fat and slice into thin (about ⅛-inch) pieces approximately 1 × 2 inches.
1 clove of garlic 1 small onion 1 citronella root (optional)	Slice the garlic, onion, and citronella into very thin circles. (If citronella is not available, just omit. There is no substitute, in this recipe.)
2 tbsp. cooking oil Medium-sized skillet	Heat the oil, then saute the garlic, onion, and citronella over high heat about one minute, stirring constantly. Add the sliced beef, continue to saute and stir over high heat another two minutes or so. The beef should still be slightly pink in spots but will mostly have changed its color. Do not overcook—it gets tough.
TO SERVE	Substitute this sauteed beef for the ground beef mixture in the recipe on page 65, and proceed as directed there.

This one-dish meal is a favorite in North Vietnam, and is the one thing that most Vietnamese in a foreign country miss the most. It is cooked in large quantities, and should either be prepared for a crowd or refrigerated and served as leftovers. The final step is completed rapidly, bowl by bowl for each individual serving and can be done at the table with an electric soup pot, or on an electric hotplate on the buffet. Be sure to have all the slicing done in advance. Variations of this recipe using chicken and pork are on pages 84 and 52.

10 lbs. soup bones and beef ribs with meat *Very large soup pot* *1½ tbsp. salt* *Water to cover and more*	Put the bones and ribs in the large soup pot and cover with water—fill the pot almost full, leaving room for boiling. Add the salt.
2 large onions *1 cinnamon stick* *1 fresh ginger root, about 3 inches long (optional)*	Chop the onions coarsely. Crush the cinnamon stick. Slice the ginger root in thin rounds. Add all to the soup pot.
	Put the pot on high heat and bring to a boil. Reduce the heat to low and simmer all day, or all night, if you have to work during the day. Add more water, if necessary, because lots of it will boil away.
3 green onions	Cut the green onions in 4-inch lengths, including tops. Put into the soup about 1 hour before serving.
1 pkg. Chinese noodles (look fun, page 17)	If fresh noodles are available, slice in ½-inch wide strips. If dried noodles are used, soak the dry noodles for 2 hours in warm water to cover. Then boil about 5 minutes, or until tender. Be sure the noodles are cooked before beginning the following steps—you just warm them up, at serving time.
SERVING DIREC-TIONS *Deep soup bowls* *Chopsticks* *Soup spoons*	Get everything ready, and ask people to come and be served before starting to do the cooking in the following steps. Be sure all the slicing is done, and every thing is laid out ready to serve. If each person watches his serving being prepared, he can prepare his own seconds—most people think it is great fun!
1 lb. fresh bean sprouts *Large pot* *3 qts. water* *Long-handled strainer*	Mix the cooked noodles with the bean sprouts. Bring the water to a boil in the pot. Put about a cupful of the noodle-bean sprout mixture in a long-handled strainer and dip into the boiling water for about a minute—just to blanch the bean sprouts and warm the noodles. Put in the bottom of an individual soup bowl.
3 large tomatoes *3 large onions* *1 lb. chuck blade roast or sirloin (tender)*	Cut the tomatoes in half, from the stem end down, then slice thin across. Cut the onion the same way, slicing very thin. Slice the beef thin (⅛-inch), in pieces about ½ inch wide and 1 or 2 inches long. Place all these on a plate or platter, arranged sepapately. Better have reserves if you have people with large appetites!
Large ladle *Chopsticks*	Put a few pieces of the beef, a couple of slices of tomato and a couple of slices of onion in the large ladle. Immerse the ladle

into the boiling soup, stir gently with the chopsticks for a minute or less—just until the beef begins to change color. It should still be pink. Then lift out the ladle, soup and all, and pour over the noodles and bean sprouts.

Chinese parsley
Fish sauce

Garnish with Chinese parsley, and put in about a teaspoonful of fish sauce, if needed, for salty flavor.

Fish sauce
Lime or lemon
Chili pepper

Serve with a side dish (small) of fish sauce to be used to add salty flavor according to individual taste. Serve large slices of lime or lemon and small shreds of fresh chili pepper, for individual garnish.

BEEF SAUTE AND STEAMED BREAD   *Four servings*

This is a kind of Vietnamese sandwich. In Vietnam where French bread has been much used for many years, this easy dish is very popular. Any type of white bread may be used.

12 slices of white bread (French, or sandwich)
Steamer

See page 10 for detailed instructions on the use of the steamer, and substitutes if you do not have one. Put the slices of bread in the top part of the steamer, not packed tightly, but arranged loosely, lying flat, so the steam can circulate between the pieces. Put over boiling water in the steamer bottom, cover and steam for about 5 minutes. Leave in the steamer, covered, until ready to serve. The bread should be soft enough to roll up without breaking, and should be warm when served.

1 lb. tender beef (sirloin or chuck blade roast)
2 citronella roots (substitute ginger root, or omit)
2 cloves garlic
1 onion (medium size)

Slice the beef thin (⅛-inch) in pieces about 1 inch wide and 2 inches long. Cut the citronella root in thin rounds. If substituting-ginger, chop very fine. Slice the garlic cloves in paper-thin rounds. Cut the onion in half from stem end down, then slice thin.

Heavy skillet
2 tbsp. cooking oil

Heat the oil on high heat. Put in the sliced beef, the citronella or ginger, garlic, and onion and saute on high heat, stirring constantly, about 2 minutes. Do not overcook—the beef should still have a few pink spots.

½ cup Onion Oil (page 28)
½ cup roasted peanuts (salted or unsalted)

Put three slices of bread on each individual plate. Pour about 1 tsp. of Onion Oil over each slice of bread. Then divide the cooked beef mixture into four parts and put one fourth over the bread on each plate. Chop the peanuts coarsely and sprinkle over the top.

TO SERVE
Leaf lettuce
Chinese parsley
Fresh mint leaves
Nuoc Mam Sauce

Serve hot, with individual small bowls for the Nuoc Mam Sauce dip. Eating instructions should be given in advance. This is eaten with the hands, like a sandwich. Roll up a slice of bread, with the beef mixture inside, along with some Chinese parsley and mint leaves. Then wrap the slice in a lettuce leaf, dip into NUOC MAM SAUCE (page 23), and eat.

NOODLES WITH BEEF AND VEGETABLES *Four servings*

Measure the vegetables after slicing or cutting.

1 cup (loose pack) Chinese cabbage (or plain head cabbage)
1 carrot
1 cup (loose pack) cauliflower
½ cup Chinese peas (or French cut green beans)

Cut the cabbage into medium-sized pieces. If Chinese cabbage is used, slice the stem pieces also. Cut the carrot in long slices, about ⅛-inch thick and 2 or 3 inches long. Cut the cauliflower flowerets in halves or thirds. Try to get similar sizes. The Chinese peas (or French-cut green beans) may be fresh or frozen.

Deep pot
¼ tsp. salt
3 cups water

Bring the water to a boil in the deep pot, put in all the vegetables and the salt and bring to a boil once more. After it boils again, start timing and cook about 2 minutes. Remove from heat and drain well. The vegetables should be almost dry when used in the following steps. Boiling quickly brings out the flavor of the vegetables and makes it easy to saute a short time and yet have them tender. Reserve the water used to boil the vegetables. It is good in soup.

1 lb. top sirloin (or other similar beef)
1 shallot (or white part of a green onion)
½ medium-sized onion

Slice beef against the grain so it will be tender. Cut into thin (⅛-inch) strips, about 1 × 2 inches. Slice the shallot and onion in thin rounds.

2 tbsp. cooking oil
Large skillet

Heat the cooking oil in the skillet, on high heat. Saute the onion and shallot, stirring, about ½ minute—just until limp, but not brown. Add the beef and saute on high heat, to turn gray. It should still be slightly pink. If it is overcooked it will be tough. Take the beef out of the skillet and set aside.

1 shallot (or white part of a green onion)
6 medium large mushrooms
1 stalk celery

Slice the shallot in thin rounds. Cut the mushrooms in half, or in quarters if larger ones are used. Cut the celery in angled slices, about 1 or 2 inches long.

2 tbsp. cooking oil

Heat the oil in the same skillet used to saute the beef. Saute the shallot about ½ minute, on high heat, stirring. Then add the mushrooms and celery and saute, stirring constantly about 2 more minutes.

¼ tsp. salt
2 tbsp. fish sauce
1 cup chicken broth (or substitute water)
Dash of monosodium glutamate

Add the salt, fish sauce, and chicken broth or plain water to the vegetables in the skillet. Bring to a boil, over high heat, then add the beef and stir well to mix. Let the mixture boil just about 1 minute then remove from heat. Keep warm until served.

½ pkg. look fun noodles (page 17)
2 qts. warm water

Soak the noodles 2 hours, or until soft. Bring to a boil and boil 5 minutes. Drain and rinse with cold running water to cool and separate the noodles. Drain well in a colander.

3 tbsp. cooking oil
Large heavy skillet

Heat the cooking oil in the large skillet, and saute the noodles on high heat about 5 minutes, stirring gently with a spatula or chopsticks. Keep everything scraped loose from the bottom.

64

There should be some slightly crisped portions. Keep warm until served.

TO SERVE	Divide the noodles into fourths, and place each fourth in a
4 deep bowls	deep Chinese noodle bowl, a soup bowl, or other deep dish.
Nuoc Mam Sauce	Spoon the beef mixture over the top. Each person stirs his own
	portion to mix. Serve with a side dish of Nuoc Mam Sauce
	(page 23) for seasoning.

NOODLES WITH GROUND BEEF   *Four servings*

This is a one-bowl meal, very good for hot weather when served with all ingredients cold. For a variation using sliced beef, see the following recipe.

1 small onion	Chop the onion and the Chinese yam very fine. Heat the oil in
1 medium Chinese yam	skillet and saute, over high heat, the chopped onion and yam,
(substitute: kohlrabi,	with the ground beef, stirring constantly until done (about 5
page 13)	minutes; do not overcook). Sprinkle black pepper on top after
½ lb. ground beef	cooked. May be served hot or cold.
1 tbsp. cooking oil	
Dash of black pepper	
2-qt. pot	If you can't find the Japanese *somen* noodles anywhere, narrow
1 pkg. somen noodles	American-style noodles may be substituted. But the dish will
(page 18)	be different. Cook the noodles in boiling water about 5 to 8
4 cups boiling water	minutes.
	Be sure to lower the heat to medium after noodles begin to boil so the pot won't bubble over. No salt or other seasoning, please. When tender, drain in a colander and rinse with cold water until noodles are cool and not sticky. Set aside.
2 cups leaf lettuce	Chop lettuce leaves into pieces about 1 inch square. Cut the
½ medium cucumber	cucumber lengthwise into about 4 slices, then slice across into
½ cup fresh bean	very thin pieces. Wash bean sprouts thoroughly in cold water
sprouts (optional)	and drain well. Chop the mint leaves and the Chinese parsley
Fresh mint leaves	coarsely. Chinese parsley may be omitted, but don't substitute
Chinese parsley (sev-	regular American parsley. The flavor is very different. Mix all
eral sprigs) (page	these green vegetables together, like a salad.
13)	
4 tbsp. roasted peanuts	Chop the peanuts coarsely, just before serving. Be sure to serve the "dust" also, since that contains much of the flavor and aroma. Don't use prechopped nuts.
TO SERVE	In each of four individual bowls (medium-size soup bowls) put
4 deep soup bowls	one-fourth of the mixed vegetables. Divide the cold noodles into four portions and put on top of the salad. Divide the cooked meat mixture into four portions and put on top of the noodles. The meat mixture may be served hot or cold. Everything else should be cold.
4 tbsp. Nuoc Mam Sauce	Pour one tbsp. Nuoc Mam Sauce (page 23) over each serving.
4 tbsp. Onion Oil	More may be added according to individual taste. Pour about one tbsp. of Onion Oil (page 28) over each serving. Sprinkle the freshly chopped peanuts over the top, and serve.
EATING INSTRUC-	Each person stirs his bowlful before eating. If not salty enough,
TIONS	add more Nuoc Mam Sauce—never add salt.

SEAFOOD MAIN DISHES

IN THIS CHAPTER are recipes using fish, shrimp, crab, and even an unusual way of preparing squid. Since Vietnam has such a long seacoast, seafoods are a major item in the diet. But since the fish and other seafood recipes are among those least liked by non-oriental foreigners, only a sampling is included in this book.

SHRIMP SAUTE

Four servings

This is another real appetite teaser. It is good picnic fare. In Vietnam it is taken on trips or picnics along with a flat cake of cooked rice—plain boiled rice that has been patted out into a flat, firm cake and which is sliced into pieces just like bread or cake when ready to eat.

1 lb. fresh (frozen) white shrimp	Wash the shrimp and remove the shells, leaving one center portion of the shell about ½ to ¾-inch wide on each shrimp. This keeps each shrimp in the original curved shrimp shape, keeps them separate and firm, and makes something nice and crunchy to chew on.
1 tsp. salt *Dash of pepper* *2 green onions*	Cut the green onions in 2-inch lengths, including the tops. Add to the shrimp, with the salt and pepper, and shake well to mix.
Small skillet *2 tbsp. pork fat (or cooking oil)*	Slice the pork fat into small, thin pieces. Note that it is easier to slice when it is chilled. Use fat trimmings from pork chops, pork roast, boiled pork, etc., for flavor. If fat is not available, substitute cooking oil. Fry the fat on high heat, stirring, about 2 minutes. Reduce heat to medium and cover. Continue to cook, covered, shaking occasionally to stir, for one more minute. Remove from heat. If using cooking oil, it should be preheated.
	Add the shrimp mixture to the cooked fat, cover, shake well to mix, put back on high heat. Cook, stirring, a few seconds. Reduce heat to medium, cover, and continue to cook about one minute.
1 tsp. sugar *½ tsp. caramel syrup* *1 tbsp. fish sauce*	Uncover skillet, stir, add sugar and CARAMEL SYRUP (page 27) and stir well. Turn on ventilating fan, add fish sauce and stir well. Cover and cook on medium heat about 10 minutes, removing cover to stir occasionally.
	Remove from heat and keep covered until ready to serve.
TO SERVE	Serve with rice. This is salty, so if it is used as a main dish it should be served with soup. It is especially good with SHRIMP AND PINEAPPLE SOUP (page 35) — the combination of the slightly acid pineapple and the salty shrimp is unbeatable.

SAFFRON FISH

A really different type of curry, a wonderful way to serve fish.

1 lb. fresh tuna, sword-fish, or other white fish	Remove bones and skin, and cut fish in small pieces (about ¼-inch thick, 2 inches square or less).
3 shallots (or white part of green onions) *2 citronella roots (substitute 1 tbsp. lemon grass powder or omit)* *½ tsp. saffron powder (substitute turmeric, or 1 tsp. curry powder)* *½ tsp. salt* *1 tsp. fish sauce* *Chili pepper to taste (optional)*	Slice the shallots and the citronella in thin rounds. Combine with the fish, along with the saffron, salt, fish sauce, and, optionally, some chili pepper, If fresh chili pepper is used, chop fine or crush. Mix together well. Let stand for 20 or 30 minutes to season.
Heavy skillet *2 tbsp. cooking oil* *1 small clove of garlic*	Heat the cooking oil in skillet on high heat. Crush the garlic clove and saute a few seconds, until the odor rises. Reduce the heat to medium, add the fish mixture and saute about 2 minutes, stirring gently so the fish will not break.
½ cup coconut milk (page 26) (substitute: 3 tbsp. heavy cream)	Add the coconut milk (or heavy cream), and stir gently. Cook about 2 minutes over medium heat. Remove from heat, and serve warm.
TO SERVE	Serve with rice, a soup, and a salad. Should be spooned over the rice, with plenty of juice.

SHRIMP AND BAMBOO STEW

7 or 8 medium-size fresh (frozen) white shrimp	Hull the shrimp, wash well, and slice in half lengthwise, removing the black vein from the back at the same time.
1 tsp. salt	Rub the salt into the shrimp well, then wash thoroughly again. The salt helps to clean the shrimp.
1-lb. can bamboo shoots	Drain the bamboo shoots and slice in varying sizes, about ⅛ inch thick.
Deep pot *4 tbsp. lard (or cooking-ing oil)* *1 tsp. Chinese shrimp sauce (page 20)* *Dash cayenne pepper* *1½ cups water* *½ tsp. salt*	Put the shrimp, bamboo shoots, and all other ingredients in a deep pot. (Lard is preferred in Vietnam for the flavor it adds. Bring to a boil and cook on high heat, uncovered, about 20 minutes.
TO SERVE	Serve hot, with rice and green salad.

CURRIED SHRIMP *Four servings*

Curry is popular throughout South and Southeast Asia. This particular curry is a real taste treat. The combination of flavorings disguise the fishy taste of the shrimp.

CURRY FLAVORING

1 heaping tsp. curry powder
1 tsp. salt
1 tsp. paprika
Dash of allspice
⅛ tsp. (scant) cayenne
Dash of black pepper
1 tsp. saffron powder (optional)
1 pinch cinnamon (or 1-inch piece stick cinnamon)

The plain curry powder only gives the nice smell and part of the nice color—the other seasonings add the special flavor. This has a much richer color and flavor than is usually seen outside the Far East's traditional curry-eating countries. The paprika and saffron powder add a richness of color that is missing in commercial curry powder. However, even commercial saffron powder is usually old enough to have lost the strength of its color. In Vietnam the saffron root is ground fresh and it gives a warm golden glow to the curry. Fresh citronella is another thing that has no real substitute. It is available in some cosmopolitan areas, and by all means try to find it; but if you can't, make the curry anyway.

1 lb. fresh (frozen) white shrimp

Use only white shrimp. Shell and devein the shrimp. To devein, slit the outside back curve of the shrimp with a sharp knife, about half way through the shrimp. Remove and discard as much of the black vein as you can get out easily. It is harmless but some people object to it. The sliced open back will cause the shrimp to open out when cooked, and it will look nicer and absorb more of the curry flavor.

1 fresh citronella root (optional)

Slice in thin rounds, then chop well. Add to the shrimp, with the curry flavoring powder. Omit the citronella if not available. There is no substitute except powdered lemon grass, which is also hard to find.

2 shallots (or white part of green onions)

Slice the shallots in thin rounds and add to the shrimp.

Deep pot with lid
2 tbsp. cooking oil

Heat the oil on high heat, reduce heat to medium and add the shrimp mixture. Cook on medium heat, stirring, about 5 minutes.

1½ cups cool water
1 tbsp. fish sauce

Rinse out the container in which you mixed the shrimp and seasonings, and pour the rinse water into the pot with the shrimp mixture. Add the fish sauce, and stir well. Increase the heat to high, bring to a boil, and let boil about 1 minute. Reduce the heat to medium.

1 tbsp. cornstarch

Mix a little of the hot liquid with the cornstarch and blend well, then add to the shrimp mixture. This will keep the cornstarch from becoming lumpy. Stir well and cook another minute or two.

¼ cup coconut milk

If fresh coconut milk or frozen coconut milk are not available, make some coconut milk using the recipe on page 26. Add to shrimp mixture, stir well, and cook another 5 minutes.

If the sauce is not quite thick enough, add a little more cornstarch, using the method described above. It should not be pasty, but should be a little thicker than water.

TO SERVE

Serve with lots of rice or noodles, and a green salad if desired. No other condiments are necessary. Chutney is not eaten with curry in Vietnam.

FRIED SHRIMP IN TOMATO SAUCE *Four servings*

This makes an excellent hors d'oeuvre, if the shrimp are cut into bite-size pieces; it is also very popular as a main dish.

2 lb. fresh (frozen) white shrimp	Shell the shrimp, and split along the back so each shrimp may be opened out flat. Use medium-sized shrimp; the small ones won't be as good.
Colander or strainer *1 tsp. salt*	Put the shrimp in a colander or strainer and sprinkle the salt over them. Rub the salt in well, to help clean the shrimp. Then wash under cool running water, rubbing gently with the hands to clean thoroughly.
½ cup flour *½ cup water* *¼ tsp. sugar* *1 tsp. salt* *Dash of black pepper*	Mix the flour, water, sugar, salt and pepper together to form a thin batter.
2 green onions	Slice the green onions in very thin rounds, including most of the tops. Add to the thin batter and mix in well.
	Put the cleaned shrimp into the batter—just dump them in all together, and stir gently to be sure that each shrimp gets well coated with batter. Leave them in the batter until you are ready to cook them.
Cooking oil *Heavy skillet or pot*	Pour enough cooking oil into a heavy skillet or pot to make the oil about ¾ inch deep. Heat the fat on high heat. Dip the shrimp out of the batter with a spoon, dipping out a little extra batter with each shrimp, and slide gently into the hot fat. Fry the shrimp on high heat, about 2 or 3 minutes on each side, or until golden brown. Remove to a wire cake cooler or similar rack to drain off the excess oil. Reserve, *uncovered*, until ready to serve. *Note:* This thin batter gets crisper and has a better taste than a thicker batter. If the shrimp are covered, they will steam and make the batter coating get soggy.
THE SAUCE *5 pickled leeks* *2 cloves garlic*	Slice the pickled leeks in thin slices lengthwise. If leeks are not available, pickled onions may be substituted. Crush the garlic thoroughly.
Deep pot *3 tbsp. cooking oil*	Heat the cooking oil in a deep pot, on high heat. Put in the pickled leeks and garlic, stir well, and saute on high heat about 1 minute, shaking the pot occasionally. When the garlic odor begins to rise, go on to the next step.
8-oz. can tomato sauce (Spanish style)	Add the tomato sauce to the garlic and pickled leeks. Cook on high heat, stirring occasionally, about 3 minutes.
1 tsp. cornstarch *1 cup water*	Mix the cornstarch and water, and add to the sauce. Stir well and continue cooking about 1 minute.
1 tbsp. fish sauce	Add the fish sauce, stir and bring to a boil. Remove from heat.
TO SERVE	Heat the sauce to a boil, drop in the shrimp and immediately remove from the heat. Serve in a bowl or on a deep plate, garnished with lettuce or parsley. Can also be eaten over rice, or as a cocktail snack.

SHRIMP IN TOMATO SAUCE   *Four servings*

1 lb. large red shrimp

Shell shrimp, wash clean, and slice open the back about half way through so the shrimp will open out when cooked. Remove as much of the vein as possible. It is not harmful, but not pretty, either.

½ tsp. salt
2 green onions
Dash of black pepper

Chop the green onions in 2-inch lengths, tops and all. Mix the onions, salt and pepper with the shrimp and let stand about 10 minutes or more.

Deep heavy pot with
* cover*
3 tbsp. pork fat (on
* 2 tbsp. cooking oil)*

Use a pot that is not too big around so the sauce won't all boil away. Chill the pork fat (scraps from pork chops, pork roast, etc.) and slice in thin small pieces. Saute fat in deep pot on medium high heat until the grease comes out.

Add the shrimp to the oil in the pot and saute on medium heat about 5 minutes, stirring often.

⅓ cup tomato sauce
* (Spanish style)*
½ cup water
1 tbsp. fish sauce

Mix tomato sauce, water, and fish sauce together and add to the shrimp in the deep pot. Bring to a boil on medium high heat, cover and reduce heat to very low. Cook about 10 minutes. Remove from heat and serve soon.

TO SERVE

Serve hot, with rice and salad. The sauce is good, too. Can be reheated.

SHRIMP AND GREEN BEAN SAUTE   *Four servings*

This is a simple and quick dish which may be used as the main dish for a simple meal, or as one of several dishes for a large dinner.

1 lb. fresh green beans

Wash the beans, then slice each bean in half lengthwise. Cut the beans into 3- or 4-inch lengths. If soft-cooked beans are preferred, frozen French cut beans may be used, slightly thawed. The crispness and sweetness of the fresh beans, however, makes this an entirely different dish.

4-qt. pot
2 qts. water

Bring water to a boil, then immerse the beans in the water in a long-handled strainer if you have one. Bring to the boil again, and cook about 1 minute, or until the beans change color, becoming greener. Remove from the boiling water at once and drain thoroughly. Set aside. Omit this step if using frozen beans.

½ lb. fresh (frozen)
* white shrimp*
1 tsp. salt

Shell the shrimp and rub the salt in thoroughly. This helps clean the shrimp. Slice each shrimp almost in half, cutting through the back. Rinse well, until clean, under cool running water.

½ tsp. salt
¼ tsp. black pepper

Mix the salt and pepper with the shrimp.

1 small onion
1 tbsp. cooking oil
Heavy skillet

Slice the onion very thin. Heat the cooking oil on high heat, then put in the onion. Saute a few seconds, stirring, until the onion smell begins to come out.

Put in the shrimp, reduce the heat to medium, and saute about 2 minutes, stirring often.

	Add the sliced green beans and continue to saute on medium heat about 5 minutes more.
2 tbsp. water	Mix in the water and fish sauce, cook one more minute and
2 tsp. fish sauce	remove from heat. If you prefer softer beans, instead of crisp ones, add ⅓ cup water and continue to cook on low heat another 3 minutes.
TO SERVE	Serve hot, with rice. Can be reheated, but is much better if eaten as soon as it is cooked.

SHRIMP FRIED RICE   *Four servings*

Here is another variation of the ever-popular fried rice, which is such a favorite way in the orient for using leftover rice. This may be made with all new ingredients, or combined with leftovers.

12 medium-sized fresh (frozen) white shrimp	Hull the shrimp, then slice each one in two or three slices lengthwise, cleaning out the black vein along the back at the same time.
1 medium onion	Cut the onion in half, then in thin slices. Smash the garlic.
2 cloves garlic	
Heavy skillet	Preheat the oil on high heat. Drop in the garlic and saute for a
3 tbsp. cooking oil	few seconds, until the characteristic odor rises. Then add the shrimp slices and onion slices. Saute, stirring constantly, on high heat about 2 minutes.
2 cups cooked rice	Since almost every Vietnamese household has leftover rice, this is a simple ingredient. You may have to cook the rice fresh, but it is better cold when used in this recipe. Reduce the heat to medium, put in the rice, and stir well, lifting from the bottom with a spatula. Cook about 3 minutes.
2 large fresh tomatoes	Cut the tomatoes in eighths and add to the mixture in the skillet. Stir gently, lifting from the bottom. Cook about 2 minutes more.
1 tbsp. fish sauce	Add the fish sauce, salt and pepper, sprinkling lightly over the
Dash of black pepper	top of the mixture in the skillet. Stir well. Turn off the heat.
¼ tsp. salt	
TO SERVE	Serve hot, with leaf lettuce, fresh mint and Chinese parsley and a side dish of Nuoc Mam Sauce (page 23).

QUICK STEAMED CRAB LOAF   *Four servings*

A new variety of meat loaf that is quick, easy, and makes a real company dish. This is called "quick" because the recipes for shrimp loaf and fish loaf involve more time for getting the fish or shrimp into paste form. This makes a good main dish, and is good for a dinner party because everything except the steaming can be done well in advance. The steaming may be done during the half hour before dinner; or it may be finished before the guests arrive and kept warm over hot water.

2 tbsp. dried tree fungus (optional, page 20.)	Soak the tree fungus and the bean thread separately about 10 minutes in warm water to cover. Cut off the hard or speckled portion of the tree fungus where it was attached to the tree.
4-oz. pkg. bean thread	Drain both bean thread and tree fungus well, and chop
Warm water to cover	coarsely with knife or shears.
2 shallots (or white part of green onions)	Slice the shallots in thin rounds. Mix with the pork. Add the chopped tree fungus and bean thread, and mix together well.
½ lb. lean ground pork	
3 or 4 oz. canned or fresh crab meat	Flake the crab meat and add to the pork mixture, kneading with the hands to mix well.
3 eggs	Mix 2 eggs and an additional egg white slightly with a fork, and add to the pork mixture. Reserve 1 egg yolk for the final step.
¼ tsp. black pepper	Add the salt, pepper and fish sauce to the pork and crab
¼ tsp. salt	mixture and mix well. The mixture should be loose and almost
2 tbsp. fish sauce	fluffy.
Steamer	Place the crab and pork mixture in a heat resistant dish, pat out
Flat 10-inch heat-resistant dish (be sure it fits steamer)	flat, and put into the top of the steamer. For instructions on the use of the steamer see page 10. Bring water to a boil in the bottom section of the steamer. Put the top section of the steamer, with the dish of crab mixture inside, in place over the boiling water, cover, and steam on high heat until the loaf is firm (25 to 30 minutes). Uncover the steamer, turn off the heat and blot the excess moisture from the top of the loaf with a paper towel. Be careful not to get a steam burn.
	Mix the egg yolk (reserved earlier) slightly with a fork, and brush all of it onto the top of the cake. Let it sit, uncovered, in the steamer for a minute or so until the yolk begins to get firm. Do not cover the steamer again, or the yolk will get too hard and will take on an "eggy" taste.
TO SERVE Nuoc Mam Sauce	Serve hot with rice, green salad, and a soup. Serve a side dish of Nuoc Mam Sauce (page 23) to dip the loaf into, bite by bite. This is good served with leaf lettuce and fresh mint leaves. Take a bite-size portion of the crab loaf, wrap it in a lettuce leaf with a mint leaf, dip into the Nuoc Mam Sauce, and eat with a bite of rice.

GREEN BEAN, CRAB AND MUSHROOM SAUTE   *Four servings*

This makes a good accompaniment for a hearty dinner, but it is also good as a light summer meal or a luncheon dish.

1 lb. fresh or frozen green beans (substitute: 1 can green beans)	Slice green beans in half lengthwise then cut in 2- or 3-inch lengths. Or use canned or frozen French-cut green beans—the Vietnamese cut them the same way. Bring water to boil, put in beans and boil about one minute, then drain. If canned or frozen beans are used, do not cook, just drain. Cut the shallots
4 cups water	in thin rounds. Preheat cooking oil in skillet and saute shallots
Medium skillet	on medium heat a few seconds, stirring. Add crab meat and
3 tbsp. cooking oil	saute, stirring, for 2 minutes. Canned crab meat may be
2 shallots (or white part of green onions)	substituted, but be sure to rinse it in running cold water, in a

3 oz. fresh or frozen crab	colander, before cooking.
10 button mushrooms ¼ tsp. salt Dash of pepper	Cut the mushrooms in half. Add mushrooms and green beans to the crab mixture in the skillet and saute for 5 minutes on medium low heat, stirring occasionally. Sprinkle salt and pepper over the top and stir well.
1 tbsp. fish sauce 2 tbsp. cold water	Mix fish sauce and cold water together, and pour over the mixture in the skillet. Stir well.
1 clove of garlic	Crush the garlic, make a hole in the middle of the mixture in the skillet and add the garlic. Let it cook a few seconds until the odor rises, then stir into the mixture. Continue to cook on medium low heat for 2 minutes.
TO SERVE	Serve hot or cold, as a main dish, or as a salad with a larger dinner.

CRAB OMELET *Four servings*

¼ lb. fresh (frozen) crab meat 1 shallot (or white part of a green onion)	Clean crab meat and flake it. Slice the shallot in thin rounds and and add to the crab meat.
Heavy skillet 1 tbsp. cooking oil	Heat oil in skillet. Add the crab meat and shallot, and saute over high heat about 1 minute or slightly less, stirring constantly but gently. Turn off heat and let the mixture cool in the skillet while beating the eggs (next step).
4 to 6 eggs	The number of eggs depends on the appetites, the size of the eggs, and the number of other dishes being served, if any. Beat the eggs with a fork until well mixed, but with the white still ropy.
¼ tsp. salt 1 tsp. fish sauce Dash of black pepper	Pour crab mixture into eggs, add salt, fish sauce, and black pepper and stir well.
1 tsp. cooking oil	Heat the oil in the same heavy skillet, over medium heat. Pour in the egg and crab mixture and stir gently with a metal spatula for about 1 minute. To stir, push the end of the spatula through the egg mixture to the bottom of the pan, then push away from you and lift slightly at the same time. This pushes the cooked mixture off the bottom of the pan and allows the liquid top portion to run down onto the bottom to be cooked.
	Reduce the heat to low and let the omelet sit in the skillet about 5 minutes. It should be firm, slightly brown on the bottom, but still very soft and partially liquid on top. Fold in half, using the spatula, and remove gently to a warm plate.
TO SERVE Nuoc Mam Sauce	Serve with rice, a salad, and a soup. A side dish of NUOC MAM SAUCE (page 23) should be served as an accompaniment to be used to individual taste. Leaf lettuce and mint leaves are especially good with this: wrap a bite of the omelet in a lettuce leaf with a sprig of mint, dip one end lightly into the Nuoc Mam Sauce, and eat with the fingers.

FRIED PORK AND CRAB ROLLS (CHA GIO)   *Six servings (52-56 rolls)*

This is a good dish for cocktails as hors-d'oeuvres, or for a meal in itself. It is a delicious dish and one of the best-remembered dishes of Vietnam. The rice paper (banh trang) used to wrap these rolls can be bought only in Vietnam (or maybe in France) and there is no substitute for it.

THE STUFFING
1 4-oz. pkg. bean thread

Soak the bean thread about 10 minutes in water to cover. Drain bean thread and chop coarsely with knife or shears.

1 medium-size Chinese yam (about 1 lb.)

Slice the Chinese yam paper-thin with vegetable peeler, roughly gather the slices and cut into fine threads.

5 green onions
1 onion
½ lb. ground pork
1 can crab meat (drained and flaked)
Pepper to taste

Chop fine both types of onion. Add the onion, the chopped bean thread, the chopped yam, the flaked crab meat, and pepper to the ground pork, and mix well after each addition. Use your hands so that the ingredients are thoroughly mixed. Substitute: You can substitute 1 cup of shelled and deveined fresh (frozen) white shrimp for the crab. Chop the shrimp well before mixing with the other ingredients.

THE ROLLING
Rice papers

Cut each sheet of rice paper in half. Trim rough edges off rice paper with scissors so that rough parts will not poke through the paper when rolling the mixture.

1 cup water
1 tsp. caramelized sugar (page 27) or 1 tsp. dark brown sugar

Mix water and sugar syrup (or brown sugar). The purpose of the sugar in the water is to make the paper turn golden brown when fried. Put half circle of rice paper on flat surface, dip your fingers in the sugared water then rub the moisture over the rice paper gently. Do not make the rice paper too wet. Let the dampened paper sit while 3 or 4 more pieces are dampened. Then begin the filling.

Fold the half-circle in half to reinforce it. Put about a teaspoonful of filling near the rounded edge in an oblong shape. Fold the sides over the filling and then roll up, gently but firmly. Put the roll aside, lying on the exposed edge of the paper. If the edge is still hard, this will soften it. See diagram on next page.

THE COOKING
Heavy skillet or pot
Cooking oil

Pour enough cooking oil into a heavy skillet or pot to make the oil about 1½ inches deep. Heat the oil on medium high heat. Slip the roll into the hot oil, the raw edge side first so that the hot oil will seal it onto the roll, then fry until golden brown. Remove to a wire cake cooler or similar rack to drain off the excess oil.

TO SERVE
Nuoc Mam Sauce
Leaf lettuce
Mint leaves
Chinese parsley
Cucumber

Serve hot, with leaf lettuce, fresh mint leaves, Chinese parsley, thin sliced cucumbers, and individual small bowls of Nuoc Mam Sauce (page 23). To eat, wrap the roll in a lettuce leaf, with mint, Chinese parsley and cucumber, and dip in the sauce.

74

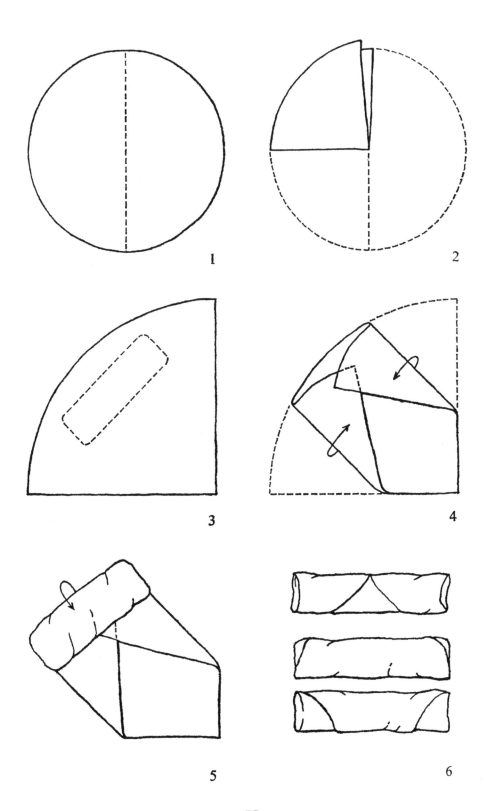

1

2

3

4

5

6

TENDER MEAT-STUFFED SQUID

Four servings

Don't just assume you wouldn't like this one. Confirmed squid-haters have taken fourths and fifths on this dish! (They often didn't know what they were eating!) The taste of squid is not there, and the rubbery consistency is gone. In fact, the squid is turned into nothing more than a handy envelope for a very tasty meat stuffing.

1 lb. fresh (frozen) squid	Clean the squid, pulling out the head with its tentacles and the insides. Reserve the tentacles. Also pull out the hard, clear bone-like spine that extends the length of the body, inside. Wash the inside thoroughly under cold running water. Chop the tentacles fine, and set aside.
½ lb. ground pork	Put the ground pork in a bowl, and add the chopped squid tentacles.
6 small (4 large) dried mushrooms *15 dried lily flowers (optional)* *Water to cover*	Soak the mushrooms and lily flowers in warm water to cover for about 15 or 20 minutes. Discard the mushroom stems, and the hard stem-end of the lily flowers. Drain well, then chop fine and add to the pork.
¼ cup bean thread *Water to cover*	Soak the bean thread about 10 or 15 minutes in warm water to cover. Measure about ¼ cup of it after it is soaked, and drain well. Chop fine, and add to the pork.
1 clove garlic *2 shallots (or white part of green onion)* *¼ tsp. salt* *1 tbsp. fish sauce* *¼ tsp. black pepper*	Crush the garlic and chop very fine; add to the pork. Slice the shallots in thin rounds and add to the pork, with the salt, fish sauce, and black pepper. Mix together well, kneading with hands.
Coarse needle *Heavy thread*	Stuff the pork mixture into the squid, packing each squid firmly full. Sew the opening shut with a coarse needle and heavy thread.
Heavy skillet *3 tbsp. cooking oil*	Heat the cooking oil in the skillet on medium heat, then add the stuffed squid. Saute about 5 minutes on medium heat, turning occasionally.
	Poke a fork into each squid so all the water can come out. Continue to cook, turning occasionally, another 7 minutes on medium heat.
TO SERVE *Lettuce* *Nuoc Mam Sauce*	Remove the thread and slice each squid in ¼-inch rounds. Keep each sliced squid together, in squid shape, if desired. Serve hot on a bed of lettuce, with lettuce peeping up between each squid. Accompany with rice, a side dish of NUOC MAM SAUCE (page 23), and soup if desired.

CHICKEN & DUCK

CHICKEN IS ANOTHER VIETNAMESE MEAT FAVORITE. Chickens are small and thus can be raised in a small area. They also produce eggs, and make themselves doubly useful. Most of these recipes call for frying chicken, rather than for baking or stewing chicken, even when the chicken is to be boiled and the meat removed from the bones. Stewing chicken often gets dried out before it is tender.

Duck, like chicken, is a universal favorite in Vietnam as well as in China. Some of the recipes included here might well be used with wild ducks brought home by a hunter. There are also some recipes for soups on pages 37, 38, and 84.

BAKED CHICKEN   *Four Servings*

This is excellent for a quick and simple dinner. Fast, but tasty enough to put before the most demanding guest. And very good for the calorie counter, too. Try taking it on a picnic. Just be sure to take plenty.

3-lb. frying chicken *½ cup soy sauce* *1 tbsp. fish sauce* *1 tsp. sugar* *2 tbsp. cooking oil* *¼ tsp. salt* *2 garlic cloves*	Cut the chicken into serving pieces. Crush the garlic, and mix with remaining ingredients to make a marinade. Pour over the chicken and let it stand at least 3 hours, or overnight, in the refrigerator.
Medium roasting pan *Aluminum foil*	Line the roasting pan with aluminum foil. Place the chicken pieces in the pan, and pour the marinade sauce over. Bake, covered with aluminum foil, in 350 F oven for about 30 minutes. Remove the foil from the top and turn the chicken. Bake another 10 minutes, uncovered. The chicken should be a golden brown.
TO SERVE	Serve with a side dish of the marinade sauce from the roasting pan. A green salad, NUOC MAM SAUCE (page 23), and rice make perfect accompaniments.

STUFFED CORNISH HEN   *Six servings*

This is true gourmet food, but won't be wasted on ordinary people.

6 Cornish hens	Clean the chickens thoroughly, wash inside and out, and dry with paper toweling. Reserve the giblets for use in the stuffing.

3 shallots (or white part of green onions) *4 cloves garlic*	Crush the garlic and shallots together.
1 cup soy sauce *1 tbsp. sugar* *¼ tsp. pepper* *3 tbsp. cooking oil* *1 tbsp. fish sauce* *Bowl large enough to hold all the chickens*	Mix soy sauce, sugar, pepper, oil and fish sauce in a large bowl, then mix in the crushed garlic and shallots. Dip each chicken into the mixture, coating each thoroughly, then put all the chickens in the bowl and let them soak for about 3 hours or longer. If the weather is hot, put them in the refrigerator.
2 cups rice *2 tbsp. butter* *1¾ cups water*	Cook POT ROASTED RICE (page 22).
1 8-oz. can straw mushrooms *2 green onions* *Giblets from 6 Cornish hens*	Chop the green onions and mushrooms coarsely. Slice the giblets very thin. If straw mushrooms are not available, fresh button mushrooms may be substituted. Do not substitute canned button mushrooms.
2 tbsp. cooking oil *¼ tsp. salt* *Dash of black pepper* *Medium-size skillet with cover*	Preheat the cooking oil in a medium-size skillet on medium heat. Put in the chopped green onions and mushrooms and the sliced giblets and saute on medium heat, stirring, about 1 minute. Cover the skillet and simmer for 8 minutes. Remove from heat.
	Mix the Pot-Roasted Rice and the sauteed giblet mixture together, and stuff it into the marinated Cornish hens. *Note:* Stuff the hens tightly, but don't handle them too much because the skin is not very sturdy. Do not try to lace or pin the opening shut—just leave it open, and if some of the stuffing falls out don't worry about it.
Large baking pan *Aluminum foil to cover*	Place the stuffed Cornish hens in the baking pan and pour the remaining marinade sauce over them. Cover the pan with foil.
	Preheat oven to 375 F. Put in the pan of Cornish hens and bake for 40 minutes.
3 tbsp. butter	Remove the foil cover and baste the hens with butter. Continue baking, uncovered, at 375 F until golden brown (about 15 minutes more).
TO SERVE	Serve on a platter, on a bed of lettuce leaves for looks. One hen is served to each individual, along with plenty of paper napkins and encouragement to use the fingers. When serving from platter to plate, try to keep the hen in the same position as it was baked in, so the stuffing won't fall out. A vegetable salad makes the perfect accompaniment.

STEAMED GINGER CHICKEN *Four servings*

If fresh ginger root is not available, use reconstituted whole dry ginger. However, it is worth taking some extra bother to try to find fresh ginger.

2 dried mushrooms (or several canned straw mushrooms)	Soak the dried mushrooms in warm water to cover about 15 minutes. Drain, remove the tough stem, and slice in very thin strips. If straw mushrooms are used, slice thin.
"Large" meat from half a frying chicken	Remove the "large" meat and skin from the bones of half a frying chicken. Reserve the bones, with the "small" meat and the giblets for soup. Cut the "large" meat into thumb-size or smaller pieces.
1 shallot (or white part of green onion) 3 thin slices fresh ginger root 1 small tomato	Slice the shallot into thin rounds. Cut the thin slices of ginger root into very fine strips. Slice the tomato (including skin) into small finger-size sections. Combine all these ingredients, and the mushrooms, with the chicken.
Small deep heat-proof bowl (cereal-bowl size) ½ tsp. sugar 1¼ tsp. fish sauce Dash of black pepper ⅛ tsp. salt 1 tsp. cooking oil	Place the chicken mixture in the heat-proof bowl. Add the remaining seasonings and oil and mix thoroughly with the hands or with a spoon.
Large heavy skillet, with cover Water	Pour about 1 inch of water into the skillet. Place the bowl of chicken mixture in the center and put the cover on the skillet. The cover should be vented, or tilted, so some of the steam can escape. Bring to a boil over medium high heat and steam until well done (about 30 minutes). Check occasionally, and if the water gets low in the skillet, add more hot water. If you have a steamer it may be used, but this is faster and easier.
TO SERVE	Serve with rice, soup, and salad.

CHICKEN AND BEAN THREAD   *Four servings*

A quick meal, simple and tasty.

2 2-oz. pkgs. bean thread Warm water to cover	Soak the bean thread in warm water to cover for at least 10 minutes. Drain and chop into medium lengths (6 to 10 inches long).
Half a frying chicken 1 shallot (or white part of green onion)	Cut the "large" meat from the bones of half a chicken, and cut into thumb-size or smaller pieces. Careful of your thumbs! Reserve the bony sections with "small" meat and the giblets for soup. Slice the shallot into thin rounds and add to the chicken meat.
Large heavy skillet 2 tbsp. cooking oil	Heat the cooking oil in skillet, and saute the chicken about 3 minutes on medium heat, stirring occasionally.
1 tbsp. fish sauce ⅛ tsp. salt Dash of black pepper ½ cup water	Add the seasonings and water to the chicken, stir well and turn the heat to high. Bring to a boil and cook for 2 minutes. Reduce the heat to medium low and cook 1 more minute. Add the bean thread, stir well to mix and cook about 1 minute. Remove from heat.
TO SERVE	Serve warm, with rice and a salad. Can be reheated, or frozen for use later.

CURRIED CHICKEN

CURRY SEASON-ING
1 heaping tbsp. curry powder
1 tsp. salt
1 tsp. red paprika
Dash of allspice
½ tsp. sugar
⅛ tsp. (scant) cayenne, dash of black pepper
1 tsp. saffron powder
¼ tsp. cinnamon (or 2-inch piece of stick cinnamon)

The plain curry powder only gives the nice smell and part of the nice color—the other seasonings add the special flavor. This has a much richer color and flavor than is usually seen outside the Far East's traditional curry-eating countries. The paprika and saffron powder add a richness of color that is missing in commercial curry powder. Unfortunately even commercial saffron powder is usually so old as to have lost the strength of its color. In Vietnam saffron root is ground fresh and it gives a warm golden glow to the curry. Fresh citronella is another thing that has no real substitute. It is available in some cosmopolitan areas, and by all means try to find it; but if you can't, make the curry anyway.

2 ½- to 3-lb. frying chicken

Cut chicken into serving pieces about 3- or 4-inch squares or rectangles; it doesn't matter.

2 fresh citronella roots (optional)
2 garlic cloves

Slice the citronella in thin rounds, then chop well. Mash garlic cloves and chop fine. Add citronella, garlic and curry flavoring powder to chicken and mix well. Let stand about 30 minutes.

Deep pot with lid
4 tbsp. cooking oil
3 shallots

Heat the oil on medium heat. Slice the shallots in thin rounds. Saute the shallots for a few seconds then add the chicken mixture. Cook on medium heat, stirring, about 10 minutes.

2 cups cool water
2 tbsp. fish sauce

Rinse out the container in which you mixed the chicken and seasonings and pour the rinse water into the pot with the chicken mixture. Add the fish sauce and stir well. Increase the heat to high, bring to boil, and let boil about 2 or 3 minutes. Reduce the heat to medium.

1 tbsp. cornstarch

Mix a little of the warm liquid with cornstarch and blend well. Then add to the chicken mixture, stir well, and cook another 5 minutes.

½ cup coconut milk

If coconut milk or frozen coconut milk is not available, make some coconut milk using the recipe on page 26. Add to the chicken mixture, stir well, and cook another 5 minutes. If the sauce is not quite thick enough, add a little more cornstarch, using the method described above. It should not be pasty, but should be a little thicker than water.

TO SERVE

Serve with rice, noodles, hot rolls, or French bread, and a green salad if desired. For additional flavoring, have a small side dish of lemon or lime juice mixed with salt. This mixture should be spread lightly over your piece of chicken.

FRIED CHICKEN CITRONELLA

This is a uniquely southeast Asian dish, and if you can't find fresh citronella (or powdered lemon grass) there is really no substitute.

½ frying chicken (about 1 lb.) with giblets	Cut the half-fryer in serving pieces. Slice the citronella and green onions in thin rounds. Add to the chicken with the salt and pepper, mix to coat the chicken, and let stand about 20 minutes or more.
3 small (2 large) citronella roots (or 1 tbsp. powdered lemon grass)	
2 green onions	
1 tsp. salt	
Dash of black pepper	
Heavy large skillet	Heat the cooking oil in the skillet on medium heat. Add the seasoned chicken and saute, stirring occasionally, a minute or so. Chop chili pepper fine and add, stirring well. Saute about 10 minutes on medium heat.
2 tbsp. cooking oil	
1-inch piece chili pepper	
1 tsp. sugar	Sprinkle the sugar and a little more black pepper over the chicken and stir well.
Dash of black pepper	
2 tbsp. chopped roasted peanuts	Be sure to chop the peanuts just before using, to bring out the flavor. Also be sure to use the "dust" from the chopping, since much of the good peanut flavor is in that. Add, with the fish sauce, to the chicken. Stir well, scraping the bottom of the skillet with a spatula if necessary. Don't let it burn. Continue to cook about 1 more minute, then remove from heat.
1 tbsp. fish sauce	
TO SERVE	Serve hot or warm, with rice or seasoned noodles. Can be used as a main dish with a regular Western meal, and is good for picnics if served still slightly warm.

TOMATO-FRIED CHICKEN   *Four medium servings*

This quick and simple dish is very good for a buffet dinner, and is easy to multiply —served with a green salad and with POT-ROASTED RICE (page 22). This is a labor-saving device for the cook and a sure way to please guests or family.

1½-lb. frying chicken	Cut the frying chicken into serving pieces. At least 1½ hours before serving, slice the shallot in thin rounds and mix with the salt and pepper. Add these to the chicken and mix thoroughly, so each piece of chicken is seasoned. Let this mixture stand at least an hour, so the seasoning can soak in. If the weather is very hot, refrigerate while soaking, otherwise room temperature is fine.
1 shallot	
¼ tsp. pepper	
1 tsp. salt	
3 tbsp. cooking oil	Heat the cooking oil in a heavy skillet, on medium heat. Put in the chicken, and fry on medium heat about 5 minutes, turning pieces of chicken once or twice. Cover and cook on medium heat another 7 minutes. Turn pieces, cover again and cook another two minutes.
Heavy skillet with lid	
2 small cloves garlic	Crush the garlic cloves with the flat side of a heavy knife, or press with a garlic press—just until the sides are broken completely. Add to the chicken, stir lightly, and allow to cook a few seconds.

2 large tomatoes *1 shallot (or white part* *of a green onion)* *1 tbsp. tomato sauce*	Chop the tomatoes coarsely. Slice the shallot in thin rounds. Add tomato and shallot, with tomato sauce, to the chicken. Stir gently, and turn the chicken pieces once. Cover, continue to cook on medium heat another 5 minutes. Uncover and turn chicken.
1 tbsp. fish sauce	Dribble the fish sauce over the chicken, stir gently, turn heat to low, and cook another minute or two. Keep warm until ready to serve.
TO SERVE	Serve hot with rice and salad—especially good with POT-ROASTED RICE (page 22). This can be cooked in advance and reheated to serve. It may be frozen, if prepared in large quantities, and it makes leftovers that taste like a banquet.

CHICKEN AND MANY VEGETABLES   *About 8 servings*

Be sure to get everything chopped and sliced before starting to cook. Though this may look complicated, it is actually easy to do. The recipe may be reduced in size, if desired, but leftovers are easy to freeze for use later.

8 dried mushrooms *Water to cover*	Soak mushrooms about 15 minutes, or until tender. Remove and discard stems. Cut each mushroom into 3 or 4 pieces.
15-oz. can bamboo *shoots*	Discard the liquid in the can. Slice the bamboo into thin (⅛ inch) pieces about 1 inch wide and 2 or 3 inches long. Irregular pieces are customary, instead of squared ones.

1 Chinese yam (sub-
   stitute: kohlrabi)
   (omit if not available)
	Peel and slice the Chinese yam (or kohlrabi) in very thin rounds.

1 small onion	Chop coarsely.
1 medium carrot	Scrape and cut into approximately 2-inch lengths. Then slice each piece into 5 or 6 thin lengthwise slices.
½ medium frying *chicken*	Wash the half chicken and cut into small serving pieces. Use the giblets, too, if you like them.

1 cup cauliflower
½ cup Chinese peas
   (substitute: French-
   cut green beans)
	You can use either fresh or frozen vegetables. Cut the cauliflower flowerets into double thumb-size pieces.

Large skillet with cover *2 cups water*	Place water in skillet, turn heat on high. Add the cauliflower and peas. When the water boils, remove from heat and drain the vegetables in a colander or strainer. Discard the water.
3 tbsp. cooking oil	Using the same skillet, heat the cooking oil on high heat. Put in the chicken and onion and saute, stirring, on high heat about 1 minute.
	Add the chopped mushrooms, and stir well. Reduce heat to medium and continue to saute, stirring, about 2 minutes.
1 tsp. salt	Add the salt, stir, and cover. Cook on medium heat about 3 minutes.
	Add the sliced bamboo shoots and Chinese yam, stir, and cover. Cook on medium heat another 3 minutes or so.

Add the carrot, stir, and cover. Cook on medium heat another 5 minutes.

Add the blanched cauliflower and peas. Stir.

¼ cup water	Mix the water, fish sauce, and monosodium glutamate (or dried shrimp, if you prefer). Pour into the skillet and stir well. Cook, uncovered, another 5 minutes on medium heat.
2 tbsp. fish sauce	
Dash monosodium glutamate (a substitute for 1 tbsp. soaked dried shrimp)	
TO SERVE	Serve hot with rice. Can be frozen, or refrigerated, and reheated.

GIBLETS AND VEGETABLES   *Four servings*

1¼ lb. cauliflower Deep pot 1 qt. water ¼ tsp. salt	Cut the cauliflower flowerets in half. Try to maintain about the same size pieces. Bring the water and salt to a boil in the deep pot. Put in the cauliflower and bring to a boil again. Boil for 3 minutes, remove from the heat and drain well. The cauliflower should be almost dry when used in the recipe.
½ lb. chicken hearts and gizzards 2 shallots (or white part of green onions)	Cut the hearts in half, lengthwise. Score the gizzards lengthwise, making 4 or 5 cuts, then slice them crosswise into ⅛-inch pieces. This helps them to cook faster and soak up more juice, and it makes the pieces look more appealing. Slice the shallots in thin rounds and add to the giblets.
10 dried mushrooms	Soak the dried mushrooms in warm water to cover about 10 minutes. Drain well. Cut off and discard the stems, and slice each of the mushrooms into four strips.
10 medium large fresh mushrooms	Slice each of the fresh mushrooms into four strips, stems and all.
2 tbsp. cooking oil Large heavy skillet with lid	Heat the cooking oil in the skillet, on medium heat. Put in the in the giblets and shallots, the fresh mushrooms and the dried mushrooms. Stir well. Saute about 1 minute on medium heat.
Dash of pepper ½ tsp. salt 1 tbsp. fish sauce	Add the pepper, salt, and fish sauce to the giblet mixture and stir well to mix. Cover lightly, letting some air get into the pan, and continue to cook on medium high heat until done, about another 5 minutes. Stir occasionally.
	Add the cauliflower to giblets and mix well. Cover and continue to cook on medium high heat another 2 minutes.
1 heaping tsp. cornstarch ⅔ cup water	Mix the cornstarch in the water so it won't get lumpy. Add to the mixture in the skillet and stir continuously, cooking another half a minute or so on medium high heat. The gravy will begin to thicken and get translucent. Remove from heat, and keep warm until served.
	NOTE: The cauliflower will still be chewy and slightly crisp. If it is cooked too long it will get tenderer, but will begin to give off that unpleasant "cabbagey" smell.
TO SERVE	Serve with rice and salad, as a main dish or one of two main dishes. Should be served warm. It can be reheated, and it can be frozen for future use.

CHICKEN SOUP-SALAD (PHO GA) *About ten servings*

This is another version of the famous combination soup and salad that is such a favorite in Vietnam. You should plan to serve this when there is a large group, because you need to make such a large quantity of soup. Of course, the soup may be refrigerated, but it really is a good excuse for a party. It is fun to let everyone get into the act, too, if it is possible to set the soup pot simmering in a place that is convenient to the table. Variations using pork or beef are described on pages 52 and 62.

THE CHICKEN SOUP
4-lb. stewing chicken
10 cups water
Beef and/or pork bones (optional)
½ stick cinnamon
10 thin slices fresh ginger root (optional)
2 green onions
Extra large soup pot

Cut the chicken in half and put into a big pot with the water. If desired, add beef and/or pork soup bones for flavor. Crush the half stick of cinnamon and drop it in the pot. Chop the ginger root fine and add. Cut the green onion in 3-inch lengths and put in the pot. Bring to a boil on high heat, then reduce the heat to medium or medium low, just enough to keep the pot gently simmering. Cook about 5 hours, uncovered, adding water as necessary to keep the level the same. If you don't add more water it will gradually boil away and you won't have any soup.

1 frying chicken
1 small onion

Cut the frying chicken in half and drop into the soup pot. Cut the onion in sixths and drop in. Continue to simmer, uncovered, until the frying chicken is tender (about 30 minutes). Test the two frying chicken halves by poking with a chopstick (or a fork, remembering that a fork is much sharper). When tender, dip out of the soup, cool, and remove the meat from the bones. Leave all the other ingredients in the soup pot. They may be eaten later, as leftovers. Set the chicken meat aside. The soup is now ready for eating at any time.

1 tbsp. salt
Dash of monosodium glutamate

Add salt and monosodium glutamate before serving.

1 pkg. Chinese noodles (look fun: page 17)

If fresh noodles are available, slice in ½-inch wide strips. If dried noodles are used, soak the dry noodles for 2 hours in warm water to cover. Then boil about 5 minutes, or until tender. Be sure the noodles are cooked before beginning to serve— just heat them up a little at serving time.

SERVING INSTRUC-TIONS
Deep soup bowls
Chopsticks
Soup spoons
1 lb. fresh bean sprouts
3 qts. water
Deep pot
Long-handled strainer

Be sure all the slicing and preparation is done in advance, then ask people to come and be served before starting to do the following cooking. Many people like to prepare their own, once they have learned the procedure.

Mix the bean sprouts with the already-cooked noodles. Bring water to boil in the deep pot, then put about a cupful of the noodle and bean sprout mixture in a long-handled strainer and dip into the boiling water for about a minute — just long enough to blanch the bean sprouts and warm the noodles. Drain a bit over the pot, then put in the bottom of an individual soup bowl.

3 large onions
3 large tomatoes

Cut the tomatoes in half, from the stem end down, then slice across in very thin slices. Slice the onions the same way.

Deep ladle	Put a couple of slices of tomato and some onion in the deep ladle. Immerse the ladle into the gently boiling soup for ½ to 1 minute only, then pour into the individual bowl. Put in plenty of soup.
Meat from the boiled chicken prepared earlier *Chinese parsley* *Lime or lemon slices* *Fresh chili pepper* *Fish sauce*	Put plenty of chicken meat on top of the soup-salad, and garnish with Chinese parsley. Serve with large slices of lime or lemon, and small slices of fresh chili pepper according to individual taste. Also serve with a small side dish of fish sauce to be used to taste if the soup is not salty enough.

MANY-COLORED CHICKEN FRIED RICE *Six servings*

This colorful dish may be cooked as indicated in this recipe, or with individual variations as a leftover to clear out the refrigerator. Each family usually has a special favorite group of things to be used with fried rice.

1 medium frying chicken	Cut the frying chicken into large pieces, for easy frying.
3 shallots *1 tsp. salt* *1 tsp. pepper*	Chop the shallots very fine. Mix with the salt and pepper, and coat the chicken pieces thoroughly with the mixture. Let the chicken stand about 30 minutes to season.
Large skillet with cover *3 tbsp. cooking oil*	Preheat the cooking oil on high heat. Add the seasoned chicken, reduce the heat to medium and cover. Cook about 10 minutes, remove cover and turn chicken. Cover and continue cooking on medium heat another 15 minutes, or until tender and slightly browned. Remove chicken from skillet, leaving whatever oil there is in the skillet.
½ lb. boiled pork or ham	Slice BOILED PORK (page 23) or boiled ham into pieces about 2 inches long, ¼ inch thick, and ½ inch wide. If canned pressed ham is used, after slicing it put it in a colander and place it under hot running water for a couple of minutes. It will have a firmer texture, the slightly slick, canned feel will be gone, and it will be pinker.
1 cup frozen mixed vegetables *3 cups boiling water*	Drop the mixed vegetables into boiling water and cook about 5 minutes. Drain well. Or substitute a cup of any leftover vegetable or combination of vegetables, if you prefer.
3 cups cooked rice	See page 21 for cooking plain rice. Use cooked rice, either hot or cold. Leftover rice is very good—in fact, cold rice is better for this recipe. Put the cooked rice in the skillet in which the chicken was fried, and saute on medium high heat about 5 minutes, stirring from the bottom with a spatula occasionally.
1 small onion	Slice the onion, and chop coarsely. Make a space in the center of the rice, drop in the onion and cook until it begins to get limp (about 1 minute) before stirring into the rice.
	Stir in the mixed vegetables and ham and cook one more minute.

2 fresh tomatoes	Chop the tomatoes coarsely and stir into the mixture. Cook another minute.
	Remove fried chicken meat from the bone, and shred it coarsely. Add to the mixture, and stir well. Cook another 2 minutes.
3 tbsp. water *1 tbsp. fish sauce*	Mix the fish sauce with the water, sprinkle lightly over the top of the rice and mix in well. Cook another 3 minutes.
2 tbsp. lard, butter, *or cooking oil* *3 cloves garlic*	This step is optional. Many Vietnamese people like more fat in their fried rice, and lard is usually the most available. Butter is also well liked, but cooking oil is probably better for you. The garlic is also optional. Make a hole in the center of the rice in the pan. Put the fat (whichever kind you prefer) into the open space. Crush the garlic cloves and put them into the fat. When the garlic aroma begins to rise, stir into the fried rice mixture and mix thoroughly. Cook another 3 or 4 minutes. Remove from heat.
TO SERVE *Nuoc Mam Sauce*	Serve hot, as a one-dish meal. May be accompanied with a soup and/or salad. Serve with side dishes of Nuoc Mam Sauce (page 23) for individual use as wanted.

CHICKEN AND BAMBOO STEW   *Four servings*

In Vietnam, fresh bamboo shoots are available during most of the year, and they are often used in preparing this dish. Dried bamboo shoots are used during the rainy season, but the dried bamboo is sun dried, for family use, and is not intended for storage beyond the three months or so of need. Dried bamboo shoots available in Chinese or other oriental stores in other parts of the world are usually machine-dried, and need considerably more soaking and boiling.

3 to 4 oz. dried bamboo
  shoots (substitute:
  15-oz. can of canned
  bamboo shoots)
3 qts. water
	Soak the bamboo shoots overnight. Next day, drain and rinse well.

Soup pot *Water* *1 tsp. baking soda*	Put the soaked bamboo shoots in a soup pot with water to cover and add the baking soda, which helps to make the shoots tenderer. Bring to a boil, and cook uncovered over medium heat about 1 hour. Drain, and rinse under running cool water, rubbing the shoots between the hands to clean thoroughly. Drain well. Cut each strip in half across, then cut each half into about 3 lengthwise strips.
2 lbs. chicken backs *and wings* *1 tsp. salt* *2 tbsp. fish sauce* *2 green onions* *Water to cover*	Return the bamboo shoots to the soup pot. Put in the bony chicken pieces. Of course a whole chicken, cut up, or any other combination of chicken parts may be used as desired. Cut onions into 2-inch lengths. Add with the salt, fish sauce, and water. Cook until everything is tender (1 or 2 hours). The bamboo shoots, when cooked, will have a slightly firm and

chewy texture, similar to that of fresh green onions. The flavor, however, is not at all like green onions.

TO SERVE	Remove the chicken bones, and serve hot with rice and a salad. This can be stored in the refrigerator several days and reheated. Also can be frozen for longer storage.
VARIATIONS	If time is pressing, the bamboo may be soaked for only three hours before the cooking process is begun. However, after soaking, draining and washing under running cool water, the bamboo shoots should be brought to a boil in water to cover. As soon as the water boils, drain the bamboo. Repeat 4 or 5 times. Then boil for 1 hour before adding the chicken.
	For a different (and good) taste, use a 15-ounce can of bamboo shoots, which need only be washed, sliced, and put in the soup pot with the bony chicken pieces and seasoning with no pre-soaking.

SHREDDED CHICKEN RICE   *Four servings*

This is a very good one-dish meal, with the rice cooked in the soup that was used to boil the chicken—an interesting technique.

2½-lb. frying chicken	Wash the chicken and cut in half.
Deep bowl *3 shallots* *2 cloves garlic* *2 tbsp. fish sauce* *¼ tsp. pepper* *¼ tsp. salt*	Crush and chop the shallots and garlic very fine. Put in a deep bowl, with the fish sauce, pepper and salt, and mix well. Then put the chicken halves in and coat them well. Let the chicken marinate in this sauce about 30 minutes or longer.
Heavy deep pot *4 tbsp. cooking oil*	Preheat the cooking oil, then fry the soaked chicken halves on medium heat about 5 minutes on each side.
1 tsp. saffron powder *(or turmeric)*	Use fresh saffron powder if available. Add and stir well. Continue to fry for another minute.
4½ cups water	Add the water, increase the heat to high and bring to a boil. After the water begins to boil, lower the heat to medium high and let the chicken cook for 15 minutes.
	Take the chicken pieces out of the soup and let them cool. Remove the meat from the bones and shred.
3 cups rice	Wash the rice and drain it. Put it into the pot with the chicken soup, and increase the heat to high. Cook, uncovered, until the water is all absorbed.
	Add the shredded chicken and stir well. Reduce the heat to low, cover, and continue to cook for 20 or 30 minutes, or until the rice is tender.
TO SERVE	Serve with leaf lettuce, Chinese parsley, fresh mint, cucumber slices, and a side dish of NUOC MAM SAUCE (page 23). Can be reheated in a steamer.

DUCK AND BAMBOO STEW   *Four servings*

This is still another variation of the CHICKEN AND BAMBOO STEW, recipe on page 86. Substitute either the bony pieces of duck, or a whole, cut-up duck. This is a good way to use tough, wild duck.

STEAMED DUCK   *Six servings*

This is considered VIP food in Vietnam. It is full of a number of delicious things, and has a flavor quite different from that of the traditional Western roast duck. When the hunter brings home a nice duck, try this for a change. You may end up buying duck to keep up with the demand! The fat and juice runs out of the duck in the steam, and the fat just seems to disappear from the meat.

20 dried lily flowers (optional) *10 dried mushrooms* *2 tbsp. dried tree fungus (optional)*	Soak the lily flowers, mushrooms, and tree fungus in warm water to cover about 20 minutes. Remove and discard the hard stem end of the lily flowers and tie each one in a knot to make it slightly more crunchy. Remove and discard the mushroom stems and slice each mushroom into 3 or 4 pieces or more, if large. Remove the black specks from the tree fungus, where it grew onto the tree. Drain well.
1½ lb. duck (part of a duck) *Heat-proof bowl*	Cut the duck meat from the bones, leaving on most of the fat. Slice the giblets in thin pieces. Put the duck and giblets into the bowl and add the mushrooms, tree fungus, and lily flowers.
4 or 5 thin slices of fresh ginger root *4 shallots (substitute: 2 whole green onions)*	Chop the ginger fine. Slice the shallots in thin rounds. Add both to the duck.
1 tbsp. rice wine	Chinese rice wine may be used or a white wine such as sauterne, but do not use Japanese sake because it is not strong enough. One tsp. of good brandy, or very good rum, may be substituted. Add to the duck.
3 tbsp. fish sauce *30 whole blanched almonds* *¼ tsp. salt*	Add the fish sauce, almonds and salt. Mix everything together well, using the hands if necessary to get the duck well coated with all the seasonings.
Steamer (page 10)	Place the bowl in the top part of the steamer, with cold water in the bottom section. Cover. Bring to a boil and steam on high or medium high heat for 30 minutes. As a substitute for the steamer, use a large skillet or pan, a small rack of any sort that will keep the bowl off the bottom, and a top that will cover tightly.
TO SERVE	Serve hot, with rice, soup, and salad. This is real gourmet fare, and should have the place of honor in any meal. Can be reheated in the steamer. Can be frozen, but should be defrosted before reheating in the steamer.

BARBECUED SAFFRON DUCK *4 small servings*

The leaves used to wrap the pieces of duck are an important part of this recipe—they tend to keep the fat from the duck out of the fire, and when fat does drip into the fire, making it flare up, the leaves protect the duck from burning. The leaves get pretty seared, but the duck huddles inside cooking in a wonderful way. Lemon leaves are by far the best, because they give some of their lemon flavor to the barbecue. But any thick, non-poisonous leaf will do the trick. Just be positive it is not poisonous, and that when burned it will not give off an unpleasant taste. Any citrus fruit leaf, guava leaf, banana leaf—in fact, any leaf of a tree with edible fruit will be good. In Vietnam, the lemon tree thorn is used as a toothpick to hold the leaf in place, having the added advantage of being green and less flammable than a toothpick. See the end of the recipe for instructions for barbecuing without any leaves at all. If wild duck is used, and the duck seems to be tough, just slice it in very fine, thin strips.

1½ lb. duck (part of a duck)	Remove the meat from the bones, using a sharp knife or cleaver. Include some of the fat, but use predominantly lean meat for this dish. Cut into medium small, thumb-sized pieces. Save the bones, bony pieces, and rest of the fat for soup; recipes on pages 29–39.
2 green onions *3 slices fresh ginger root* *2 cloves garlic* *1 tsp. saffron* *Dash of black pepper* *1 tbsp. soy sauce* *1 tbsp. fish sauce* *1 tsp. sugar* *1 tbsp. cooking oil*	Chop the onions, fresh ginger root, and garlic very fine. Add to the duck, in a bowl. Citronella or lemon grass may be substituted for ginger, if you have it. Add all the seasonings to the duck, and mix together well with the hands. Let it stand and marinate 20 minutes or more. If the weather is too hot, store in the refrigerator.
Large lemon leaves	Wrap each piece with a lemon leaf or if very thin strips of duck are used, bunch several together. Fold the tip of the leaf over the meat, then the stem end, leaving the sides open. If the leaf won't stay folded, break the central stem by folding firmly. Keep together with a toothpick or other less flammable pick. Try the Vietnamese method of using lemon thorns, if you have the time to cut them off the tree.
Folding sandwich grill or other barbecue equipment *Barbecue grill*	Place the wrapped duck in a folding wire sandwich or hotdog cooker, and place over hot coals. Barbecue, turning occasionally, until done (about 15 minutes). When the fat drips out, the fire will flame up, but the leaves will protect the duck.
TO SERVE	Serve hot, with rice. Each person unwraps his own duck and puts it on top of his rice. Put a plate or bowl in the center of the table for the leaves—don't keep track of individual appetites!
VARIATION	If non-poisonous leaves are not available, or the group is too hungry to wait until a test is made, regular long skewers may be used. Put the pieces of duck, folded, packed close together on the skewer. Broil over low coals, turning frequently. Watch carefully, and if the fire flames up from dripping fat, or for any other reason, don't let the duck burn.

TURNIP-PATCH DUCK   *Four servings*

This dish rather effectively disguises the strong flavor of turnips and the strong flavor of duck, making a pleasant surprise for the duck-hunter or the housewife with leftover duck.

1 lb. of duck (part of a duck)	Cut the duck meat off the bones and slice thinly, including some fat with the lean. Use the giblets, if you have them, sliced thin. The pieces of duck should be about ¼ inch thick or less, and 1 inch wide and perhaps 2 inches long: irregular pieces are to be expected.
Large skillet with cover *2 tbsp. cooking oil*	Heat the cooking oil in the skillet on high heat, and then saute the duck, stirring constantly, for about 3 minutes. Remove from skillet and set aside.
2 medium-size turnips (about 1 to 1¼ lb.)	Pare the turnips and cut off root and stem ends. Cut into large finger-size chunks, about 2 or 3 inches long.
2 tbsp. cooking oil	Using the same skillet as for the duck, heat the oil on high heat and saute the turnips, stirring frequently, about 5 minutes.
1 clove garlic	Crush the garlic, chop fine, and add to the turnip. Stir well. After a few seconds, when the garlic begins to make its presence known, put in the sauteed duck. Stir well.
1 tbsp. fish sauce *1 tsp. salt* *1 cup water*	Add the fish sauce, salt and water and stir well. Bring to a boil on high heat, cover, and reduce the heat to medium low. Simmer about 1 hour, or until duck and turnips are tender.
TO SERVE	Serve hot, with rice, soup, and salad. Garnish with Chinese parsley, if available.

BARBECUED WHOLE DUCK   *Four servings*

This duck has a wonderful flavor, and is one of the simplest of meals to prepare. It needs one hour marinating and two hours cooking time, but need not be watched, except for the last 30 minutes. This is ideal for the outdoor rotisserie, because it needs the charcoal flavor. The lime or lemon leaves and citronella leaves give it a special flavor, too; but the substitution of celery tops and parsley will not make it taste bad! It will have a different flavor, but an excellent one.

4-lb. duck (wild tender one, or Long Island)	If the duck is frozen, thaw it before beginning anything. Wash thoroughly inside and out, and pat dry. Remove the giblets, and reserve for another recipe or for soup.
2 tbsp. cinnamon *2 tbsp. salt* *1 tbsp. sugar* *¼ tsp. black pepper*	Mix the cinnamon, salt, sugar, and pepper, and divide into three equal parts. Use one-third of the seasoning to rub the inside of the bird thoroughly, massaging it in well, and use the second third to rub into the bird's skin. Let the bird soak up the seasoning for an hour or so. The remaining third is used later.
Charcoal brazier *Electric rotisserie*	Start a charcoal fire, and let the coals get fairly hot.

Lime or lemon leaves
Citronella leaves
* (substitute: celery*
* tops and parsley)*

Stuff the duck loosely with the leaves. Don't chop them up—use whole leaves. Sew or skewer the bird tightly closed. Put it on the rotisserie skewer and place over coals. Start the rotisserie going, and broil over medium hot charcoal 1½ hours.

⅓ cup water
Basting brush

Add water to the remaining third of the seasoning mix. Baste the duck with this sauce about every 5 minutes, cooking for another 30 minutes.

Remove the rotisserie skewer with the duck, and let it cool enough to be handled. Open up the duck, remove and discard leaves. Chop the duck into small bite-size pieces with a cleaver or carve it into large serving-size pieces, if desired.

TO SERVE

Serve with soup, salad, and rice as a main dish. If the fat and skin is not popular, save it and make duck and bamboo stew, or saute it.

SALADS

FRESH LEAF LETTUCE, fresh mint leaves, Chinese parsley, and fresh chives make an excellent accompaniment for any Vietnamese meal. Note, too, the several recipes for SOUP-SALADS on pages 52, 62, and 84.

PICKLED BEAN SPROUTS
Four servings

This is very good for lunch on a hot day. Serve with cold BOILED PORK (page 23), NUOC MAM SAUCE (page 23), and rice; or with PORK STEW (page 40).

1 lb. fresh bean sprouts
1 medium carrot
1 green onion
1 bamboo shoot
  (canned)

Wash the bean sprouts and drain thoroughly. Canned bean sprouts won't do. Shred the carrot. Add to bean sprouts, in large bowl. Cut the green onion, including the top, into 2-inch lengths. Then slice into lengthwise strips. Slice the bamboo shoot very thin, about 1/16 inch, then cut into small strips. Be sure to use a Chinese bamboo shoot. If desired, a small can of presliced bamboo shoot can be substituted, but it should be well drained and rinsed with cold water.

1 tbsp. rock salt
Water

Regular salt may be used. Mix all ingredients together, including the salt, and pour in water to cover. Let the mixture stand at room temperature at least three hours, but preferably all day. This will keep about two days in the refrigerator.

PICKLED BEAN SPROUTS WITH BOILED PORK
Four servings

Medium pot with cover
1 lb. pork leg or belly
Cold water to cover

Pork may be lean or fat, depending on personal preference. Since the pickled bean sprouts are slightly sour, some people like more fat in the pork. Place the pork in the pot, and pour in cold water to cover. Bring to a boil, then lower heat and cover the pot. Let the meat simmer until done (about 20 minutes). To test, push the end of a chopstick into the meat. If it goes in easily, the meat is done. Remember, a fork is much sharper than a chopstick, so a fork-test for doneness is quite different. Do not overcook the meat; it should be well done but firm.

92

If you discover it is still too pink or tough inside when you begin to slice it, just put it back in the pot and boil some more. Remove the pork to a plate or platter and let cool to room temperature. When thoroughly cool, cut across the grain into thin (1/16-inch) slices. Then cut the slices into pieces about two inches square.

TO SERVE
1 lb. pickled bean
*   sprouts*

Drain the pickled bean sprouts (page 92) and pile in the center of a large plate or medium-size platter. Arrange the cold sliced pork artistically around the edges so that it will be easy to serve.

Nuoc Mam Sauce

Place Nuoc Mam Sauce (page 23) in small bowl with serving spoon. A gravy bowl and gravy ladle works very well for this. Place hot rice in another bowl with serving spoon or wooden paddle.

EATING INSTRUC-
*   TIONS*
Individual place set-
*   ting:*
1 tiny sauce dish
1 rice bowl
Chopsticks

Serve rice in individual rice bowls, and a spoonful of Nuoc Mam Sauce in individual sauce dishes. Each person takes a chopstickful of pickled bean sprouts and places it on top of his rice. Then he takes one piece of cold sliced pork, dips it into the sauce, places it on top of the pickled bean sprouts, and eats with rice.

CUCUMBER SALAD

Though this is called cucumber salad, there are many other goodies in it as well. It is delicious as a one-dish meal on a hot day, or may be served as a salad with dinner. Good for picnics, a dieter's delight, the complete all-purpose food.

2 large cucumbers
1 tsp. salt
Water to cover

Slice the cucumbers paper thin (use the wide slicing section on your grater, if it has one; or use a vegetable parer). Soak the thin slices in salted water to cover about 30 minutes or more. Drain through a piece of nylon net and twist to squeeze water out thoroughly.

½ lb. boiled shrimp
*   (page 24)*

Cool the shrimp thoroughly. Slice in halves or thirds lengthwise.

½ lb. boiled pork
*   (page 23)*

Slice pork in thin (¼-inch) pieces, about finger-size or slightly smaller. Cool thoroughly.

1 or 2 tbsp. Nuoc Mam
*   Sauce (page 23)*

Mix cucumber, shrimp and pork together. Add less than 1 tablespoon Nuoc Mam Sauce and taste—every taste is different. Add more, as you like.

3 or 4 tbsp. sesame
*   seed*

Roast the sesame seed slightly in a small covered pan on top of the stove, shaking to keep from burning. Then crush slightly to bring out the flavor. Add to the salad just before serving and mix in well.

About 20 mint leaves

Chop the mint leaves coarsely and add to the salad.

TO SERVE

Serve in small bowls, as a main dish for luncheon or other light meal; or as salad with a dinner.

93

GREEN VEGETABLE SALAD

Any green vegetable, in season, may be served alone or in combination with others. Serve with a side dish of NUOC MAM SAUCE (page 23) for seasoning. Especially good with most Vietnamese dishes is a combination of leaf lettuce, chives, Chinese parsley, fresh mint, and cucumber. Cabbage leaves are also good. Let personal preference be your guide.

GREEN PAPAYA SALAD   *Four servings*

This is included for the benefit of those lucky people who are able to get green papaya. A variation using turnips (also delicious) is included for the others.

2 cups (packed) green papaya	(The number of papayas used will vary, depending on the size.) Use papayas that are still very hard and bright green. Peel the papayas, and shred in long slender shreds on a grater. Use just the green meat—stop when the seeds in the center appear. Put into a serving bowl or platter.
½ lb. boiled fresh pork (page 23) *⅓ lb. boiled shrimp (page 24)*	Slice the boiled fresh pork in thin (⅛ inch) slices, about ½ inch wide and 1 inch long. If the shrimp are small, slice in half lengthwise. If large, slice in thirds lengthwise. Put pork and shrimp on top of the papaya, arranged nicely.
3 tbsp. fresh mint leaves *Nuoc Mam Sauce*	Chop the mint leaves coarsely and sprinkle over the salad. Pour over 2 or 3 tablespoons of the NUOC MAM SAUCE (page 23), to taste. When ready to serve, mix together.
TO SERVE	Serve as a light luncheon, with tea and perhaps soup, or serve as a salad accompaniment to a large dinner.

TURNIP SALAD   *Four servings*

This is a variation of the green papaya salad, but is delicious in its own right. Be sure to use young and crisp white turnips.

2 cups (packed) shredded white turnips	The number of turnips used will vary, depending on the size. Wash the turnips thoroughly, then scrape off the skin. Shred, on a grater, in long thin shreds. Put into a serving bowl or on a platter.
½ lb. boiled pork *⅓ lb. boiled shrimp (page 24)*	Cut the BOILED FRESH PORK, preferably fresh ham, (page 23) in thin (⅛-inch) slices about ½ inch wide and 1 inch long. If the shrimp are small, slice in half lengthwise. If they are large (don't use the extremely large ones), slice in thirds lengthwise. Put the pork and shrimp on top of the shredded turnip, arranged nicely.
3 tbsp. fresh mint leaves *Nuoc Mam Sauce*	Chop the mint leaves coarsely and sprinkle over the top of the salad. Pour over 2 or 3 tablespoons of NUOC MAM SAUCE (page 23), to taste. When ready to serve, mix together.
TO SERVE	Serve as a light luncheon, with tea and perhaps soup; or serve as a salad accompaniment to a large dinner.

CHICKEN SURPRISE SALAD

This chicken salad is certain to surprise—and to please. It is very good for picnics, for light summer meals, for a salad accompaniment to a soup or stew, and is a dieter's delight.

½ boiled frying chicken
1 small head cabbage

Chill the BOILED CHICKEN (page 24) and shred it. Shred the cabbage or slice very fine with a sharp knife. Mix the chicken and cabbage together lightly.

About 20 fresh mint leaves
3 or 4 stems Chinese parsley (optional)

Chop the mint leaves and the Chinese parsley coarsely. Mix lightly with the chicken and cabbage.

Nuoc Mam Sauce to taste

Add NUOC MAM SAUCE (page 23) to taste—start with about a tablespoonful.

TO SERVE

Serve alone with tea, or with rice, or as a salad accompaniment to a main dish or a stew. It should be cool, but not necessarily chilled.

PORK RIND SALAD
Four servings

An inexpensive, and diet-conscious, salad that is quick and easy to make and is very tasty. The butcher will probably be happy to give you some pork skin to try this with.

1 cup pork rind (fresh pork skin)
Water to cover

Boil pork rind in water to cover about 20 minutes. Rinse in cold water to cool and drain well. Remove excess fat from the skin, and slice into thin slivers about the same size as bean sprouts.

1 lb. fresh bean sprouts
Hot water to cover

Wash and clean bean sprouts, then soak about 5 minutes in hot water to cover. Drain well.

2 star fruit (star apple or carambole)
SUBSTITUTE:
1 small cucumber
1 tbsp. lime juice
Water to cover

Peel star fruit, and slice into thin slivers, same size as bean sprouts and pork rind. Drain well. If star fruit is not available, cucumber soaked in lime-flavored water may be substituted. Peel the cucumber and slice into thin slivers the same size as the bean sprouts. Then soak the slivers in the lime juice and water to cover for about 10 minutes and drain well. This gives the slightly acid flavor characteristic of star fruit.

¼ cup mint leaves
¼ cup Chinese parsley (if available)

Chop mint and Chinese parsley leaves coarsely. Reserve.

2 tbsp. sesame seeds

Roast the sesame seeds and crush slightly in a mortar. Reserve.

2 tbsp. Nuoc Mam Sauce (or to taste)

Combine the pork rind, bean sprouts, star fruit (or cucumber), mint, and Chinese parsley. Toss with NUOC MAM SAUCE (page 23) until well mixed. Keep cool until served.

TO SERVE

Toss salad with crushed sesame seed just before serving. If the seeds get soggy, the nice smell and good flavor are dissipated. Serve as a light salad meal, or as a salad course for a larger meal.

SALAD "SANDWICH"

This particular item of Vietnamese food is one of the most versatile. It is very good served as hors d'oeuvres, in a small bite-size bundle. It makes wonderful picnic fare, with each person making his own "sandwiches." And it also is good for a complete meal, especially served with soup. Since all the ingredients are served cold, it may be prepared well in advance of serving time.

½ lb. udon noodles *2 qts. water*	Bring the water to a boil and put in the noodles. Boil about 5 minutes, then drain and rinse under cool running water. (The noodles will be sticky, and will have to be pulled apart in lumpy bunches when served.) Put on a bed of lettuce leaves to serve.
1½ lbs. boiled shrimp *(page 24)* *1 lb. boiled pork* *(page 23)*	Cook shrimp and pork according to Basic Recipes. It takes about 30 minutes for the pork, only 3 or 4 minutes for the shrimp. Slice the shrimp in 2 or 3 lengthwise pieces, depending on how large the shrimp are. Slice the pork in small pieces, about ¼ inch thick and 2 inches square, or smaller. Arrange the sliced pork around the edges of a serving plate or platter, with the sliced shrimp in the middle.
4 lb. leaf lettuce *Chinese parsley* *Chives* *Fresh mint leaves*	Wash and drain all the vegetables. Serve on a large platter or bowl, each in a separate pile; or on individual plates or bowls.
Nuoc Leo Sauce	Be sure to have enough NUOC LEO SAUCE (page 23) so that each person can have about half a cupful of it, in individual bowls.
TO SERVE	Each individual can make his own "sandwich" by taking a leaf of lettuce and putting on a little of each of the ingredients shown above except the sauce, wrapping the lettuce leaf more or less firmly around them, and dipping up some Nuoc Leo Sauce with one end of the bundle. If it falls apart into the sauce, just fish it out with your chopsticks or a fork.
HORS D'OEUVRE *Green onion tops* *Boiling water*	Cut the tops from a bunch of green onions. Wilt the onion tops quickly by dipping into boiling water just enough to make them limp. If the tops are fairly wide, cut them in half lengthwise before wilting them.
	Make small "sandwiches" by spreading a small amount of the noodles on a lettuce leaf, then putting in a small amount of each of the other ingredients. Fold over each end of the lettuce leaf, then roll up firmly (but be gentle so the leaf won't disintegrate). Tie each bundle with a wilted green onion top. Serve with Nuoc Leo Sauce.

DESSERTS

VIETNAMESE SWEETS ARE QUITE DIFFERENT from those outside the orient. Sweets are served with tea whenever a guest comes to visit, but are not necessarily considered a part of a meal. Fresh fruit, in season, is a basic part of Vietnamese eating. And there are many fresh fruits, some of which, unfortunately, are not available outside the tropics.

PRINCESS CAKE
Twelve servings (or six?)

This recipe was reconstructed from a childhood memory of a cake baked by my mother. It had been long forgotten, but suddenly one day came to mind and through a few experiments the Princess Cake of my childhood has come to be written in English. These actually are either very small cakes or very large cookies. There is nothing really like them except that small cupcakes or petit fours resemble them in size. The completed cake looks like a small crown, with the inside layer peeking through the outside portion. The inside is much like shortbread; the outside is more like a crisp, rather hard cookie. The outside dough may be left plain, or may be colored any color desired.

INSIDE DOUGH
1 cup flour
8 tbsp. vegetable shortening

Sift the flour. Melt the shortening (the Vietnamese use lard; unsalted butter may be substituted). Mix shortening and flour together thoroughly, until crumbly, *before* adding sugar, in order to kept this dough crumbly.

½ cup sugar
2 or 3 drops of banana extract

Knead the sugar and banana extract into the mixture, mixing until it will barely hold together. If it won't hold together, add a little more shortening.

Divide the dough into 12 equal portions, and roll each portion between the hands into a smooth ball.

OUTSIDE DOUGH
1 cup flour
½ cup sugar
3 tbsp. shortening

Sift the flour. Mix in the sugar. Melt the shortening, and mix into the flour and sugar. In this case the sugar is mixed with the flour to make this dough firmer than the inner dough, above.

1 tsp. banana extract
½ tsp. green (or other) food color
4 tbsp. water

Mix the banana extract and the food coloring with the water, then add gradually to the flour mixture, kneading with hands and folding until thoroughly mixed. Roll between the hands to make a rope about a foot long, then fold the rope and roll again. Repeat this several times.

97

Divide the outside dough into 12 equal portions and roll each portion into a smooth ball. Then pat out between the hands, shaping with the fingers, to make a circle large enough to envelop a ball of the inside dough. Wrap each ball of "inside dough" in a circle of "outside dough," pulling the edges together and patting smoothly so that it becomes a smooth, colored ball.

2 sheets of paper
Cookie sheet

Typing paper, or other similar paper, should be used. Do not use waxed paper. (Cakes of this sort are traditionally cooked and served on white paper.) Cut the paper into 3-inch squares, and place a ball of dough in the center of each square, placing about 2 inches apart on a cookie sheet.

With a sharp knife, make a cut across the top of each ball, cutting about ¼ of the way through the ball. Then make two cuts, much shallower, on each side of the deep cut. The top of the ball should look as if it is marked in six pie-wedge pieces. If the cuts are too deep the cakes will fall apart while cooking; if too shallow, the "crown" won't open up enough. If the shallower cuts are made across the first deep cut, the shape will be distorted.

1 tbsp. sesame seed

Sprinkle sesame seeds over the top of each cake.

Preheat oven to 350 F. Bake cakes about 25 minutes. The tops will gradually spread open, and the tips will be slightly brown.

TO SERVE

Serve warm or when cooled, like cookies. Very good with tea.

COCONUT AND SESAME FILLING

This wonderful dessert filling is a favorite in the orient, and among the fortunate people outside the orient that have had an opportunity to taste it. It is not difficult to make, and will generously repay all effort. Use in the next two recipes.

3 tbsp. sesame seed
Heavy skillet with
    cover

Toast the sesame seed in a heavy skillet on top of the stove, shaking and stirring often to keep from burning. Use medium heat. It will take 3 to 5 minutes, depending on various factors. Remove from skillet to stop roasting. The seeds have a much nicer flavor when toasted—in fact, they are almost flavorless unless they are toasted.

1 fresh coconut
    (substitute: 1½ cups
    sweetened bakers
    coconut)

Remove the meat from a fresh coconut. See page 14 for easy instructions. Grate it coarsely and toast in the same heavy skillet, stirring constantly, on medium heat, about 1 minute.

1 cup sugar
1 tbsp. water

Add sugar and water and continue to stir on medium heat about 3 minutes. *Note:* If sweetened baking coconut is used, reduce the sugar to ½ cup.

Add the sesame seeds and continue to stir over medium heat another 2 minutes. The sugar will melt, coating the coconut and sesame seeds.

Remove from skillet to a bowl, and use as directed in recipes on pages 99–100—or find your own uses for it. Refrigerate, if it is not all used immediately. This will keep in the refrigerator a month or so, or it can be frozen.

SOFT CAKE WITH COCONUT-SESAME FLAVORING

This Vietnamese cake has many versions. It is very soft, almost like dough, but very tender. Easy to eat, with a gentle flavor, it is an ideal end for a heavy dinner. It is also good served in the afternoon with tea.

1½ cups glutinous rice powder or flour 1½ cups water (or milk, if desired)	Mix the rice flour and water or milk together thoroughly with a spoon. If you use a stainless steel bowl, the dough won't stick to the sides so much. This will make a sticky dough.
Teacloth or other close-woven cloth	Dampen the cloth, place the lump of dough in the center and wrap well. The shape doesn't matter at this stage.
Steamer (see page 10)	Put hot water in the bottom section of the steamer. Place the wrapped dough in the top section, put the top section in place and cover. Steam over high heat 30 minutes. Be sure not to run out of water in the bottom of the steamer. Remove the dough from the top of the steamer (be careful not to get a steam burn), unwrap it, using tongs or gloves if necessary. Put the steamed dough back into the stainless steel bowl.
1 cup sugar ½ cup water Deep pot	Put the water and sugar in the deep pot and stir well. Bring to a boil, on high heat, and boil about 2 or 3 minutes or until it makes a light sugar syrup.
½ cup candied fruit (preferably squash, page 103)	Break the candied fruit into small pieces, about thumbnail size or smaller. Stir into the sugar syrup.
	Pour the sugar syrup and the fruit into the bowl with the dough, adding gradually and stirring into the dough.
¼ cup coconut-sesame seed filling	Stir in the COCONUT-SESAME FILLING (page 98). The dough will be quite sticky.
10-inch cake pan About ¼ cup potato flour	Sprinkle the potato flour generously over the bottom of the cake pan. Put the cake mixture into the pan, and begin to pat it out flat. Sprinkle more potato flour over the top of the cake and continue to pat gently and rub the flour into the surface of the cake. It should finally be smooth on top and fill the cake pan.
	Let the cake cool well. When it is cold, cut into squares, fingers, or whatever shape your whim dictates. It will still be somewhat sticky and dough-like in texture but very tender.
Potato flour	Sprinkle potato flour generously in another pan. Roll the cut pieces in potato flour, coating well so the cake will not be sticky to handle. The potato flour is easy to digest raw, unlike other flours, and will not get sticky.
TO SERVE	Serve cold, with tea.

FRIED SWEET BALLS

THE DOUGH *¾ cup water* *¼ cup sugar*	Mix water and sugar, bring to a boil, stirring only until sugar is dissolved. Remove from heat and let cool.
10 oz. (1½ cups) *glutinous rice flour*	Mix the sugar syrup with the flour, stir and mix well. It will be about the consistency of pie dough.
STUFFING *Cooking oil* *Coconut-Sesame Filling*	Put a small amount of cooking oil on the palms of the hands, and take out a piece of the dough large enough to form a ball about 1 inch in diameter. Roll the dough between the hands until a ball is formed. Then flatten it carefully with the fingers and palms, making a circle about 3 inches across. Put a teaspoonful of Coconut-Sesame Filling (page 98) in the center, and fold the edges up, pinching together closely. Carefully roll between the palms again, making a filled ball. Be sure to get all the openings closed—otherwise the ball might explode when it is fried. Thin places in the dough may also cause small explosions. Stand back when frying!
Deep fat (3 inches)	Drop the balls into hot deep fat about 3 at a time and fry until golden brown. Drain on paper towels.
	If too many balls are fried at the same time, they will stick to each other. If too much sugar is used in the dough, it will burn easily. If the balls are put in when the fat is not hot enough, they will stick to the bottom of the pan.
TO SERVE	Like doughnuts, these are best served hot. Warn people not to burn tongues on the hot filling! But, also like doughnuts, they are tasty when they are cold.

BANANA CAKE

2 lb. bananas *(very ripe)*	Peel bananas and smash them with flat side of heavy knife. Put into mixing bowl.
½ cup heavy cream *1 cup milk* *1 cup flour (sifted)* *½ cup sugar* *Pinch of salt*	Add cream, milk, flour, sugar, and salt to bananas and mix thoroughly. If available, substitute one cup coconut milk for the heavy cream and milk. Coconut milk gives a better texture and flavor, and more moisture than regular cows' milk. (See pages 15 and 26, "coconut milk.")
9-inch cake pan *Cooking oil* *1 tbsp. flour*	Oil the cake pan, then put in flour. Shake flour around to coat sides and bottom of pan, then pour out excess flour. Pour banana mixture into pan, and bake at 350 F until golden brown on top (about 1 hour).
TO SERVE	May be served hot or cold; good with tea.

FANCY BANANA CAKE WITH CASHEWS   *Two one-layer cakes*

This soft cake is considered a real luxury item by foreigners, but in Vietnam, where bananas and coconuts are plentiful, it is not such an expensive dish.

3 eggs 1 cup sugar	Break the eggs into mixer bowl and add the sugar. Set the mixer on low speed and blend the sugar and eggs thoroughly. Then turn the speed to medium setting for about 2 minutes or until the mixture is a pale yellow and gets fluffy. Do not use a high speed on the mixer, since the slow beating gives the same effect as beating by hand—getting lots of air in and making things stay tender.
¾ cup whipping cream	This is a substitute for fresh coconut milk. Pour the cream into the mixing bowl with the eggs and sugar and continue to beat for a few seconds, just enough to mix thoroughly. If you beat too long you will have butter.
1½ cups flour	Sift the flour after it is measured. Dump all the flour into the mixing bowl with the egg and sugar and cream mixture and stir with a wooden spoon just until mixed (about half a minute.)
4 lbs. very ripe bananas	Peel the bananas, and smash each one with the flat side of a heavy knife or cleaver. Just give one good smash to each banana, don't mash them up into a gooey mess. Add to the batter without stirring.
¾ cup chopped cashew nuts	Chop the cashew nuts coarsely. Add to the batter.
1 cup shredded fresh coconut	If fresh coconut is not available, packaged sweetened coconut may be substituted. The cake will be sweeter, but it will be good. Add the coconut to the batter. Stir just until everything is well mixed together.
2 8-inch cake pans Oleomargarine or butter Flour	Grease the cake pans thoroughly, with oleomargarine or butter. Sift in some flour and shake the pan around so that sides and bottom are well coated. Pour out the excess flour.
	Preheat the oven to 350 F.
	Pour the batter into the cake pans and bake on center rack about 55 minutes or one hour. The top should be golden brown.
TO SERVE	Slice and serve warm or cold. The flavor and texture is different, but it is very good both ways. This is not a light, fluffy cake; it is a very tender, solid pudding-like cake.

ALMOND COOKIES

This oriental favorite is not exclusively Vietnamese—its origin was probably China and it is best known in the Western world as a dessert served in Chinese restaurants. It is really quite simple to prepare and can be relatively inexpensive. Be sure to hide the cookie jar!

1 cup blanched almonds (substitute: cashews) 2 cups sifted flour 1 scant cup sugar (or less) 1 tsp. baking soda 1 tsp. salt (omit if salted nuts are used)	Chop the nuts very fine in a nut chopper. Sift the flour with the soda, sugar, and salt and add the nuts. Mix together thoroughly.

1 cup Crisco (or other vegetable shorting) (for a real treat, substitute the juice squeezed from fresh grated coconut)	Mix in the shortening a small amount at a time, rubbing between the hands. The dough will finally begin to stick together. Shape the dough in any way you wish. Traditional shapes are flat, round cookies—anywhere from 1 to 4 inches across; or small balls that will flatten out slightly when cooked. If coconut milk is used, the cookies will be more the texture of oatmeal cookies.
Whole almonds (with skin still on) (substitute: whole cashews, if cashews are used in the basic recipe) *Cookie sheet*	Place the cookies on a cookie sheet, about an inch apart, and gently press an almond into the center of each one. Bake in 350 F oven about 20 minutes. The almond cookies should not be brown, but if cashews are substituted the cookies will be slightly brown. Cool on wire rack. Store in airtight container.

CARAMEL RICE PUDDING *Six to eight servings*

A quick and easy dessert that may be varied with seasonal fruits or served with chilled canned fruit or fruit salad.

4 tbsp. sugar *2-qt. mold*	Put the sugar in the mold and put on high heat, for just a few seconds. Be sure mold will fit into the steamer used below.
1 tbsp. water	Add 1 tbsp. or less of water—just enough to dampen the sugar. Return to stove, on high heat, and cook until a spot of brown shows somewhere. Then lift the mold off heat and quickly tilt and turn in a circular motion. The brown will quickly spread all over. Return to the heat occasionally, and continue to tilt and turn until it is evenly dark caramel in color. It will be a thin syrup. Cool, occasionally tilting and turning to coat the bottom of the mold and the sides slightly.
½ cup glutinous rice *½ cup plain rice* *3 cups water* *Heavy 3-qt. pot*	Put the two kinds of rice and the water into the pot, over high heat, and bring to a boil. Reduce the heat to medium low, cover, and cook until all the water is absorbed. Remove from heat.
Large mixing bowl *6 heaping tbsp. sugar*	Pour the rice into a large mixing bowl, add the sugar and mix well.
⅔ cup milk *3 eggs*	Add the milk. Break the eggs into the mixture, and mix together well with a spoon.
Steamer, or large skillet with cover *Water*	Pour the pudding mixture into the caramel-coated mold. Place in a steamer (see page 10), or use a large skillet with cover. Place water in the skillet, about 1½ inches deep, put the mold in the water, and cover.
	Bring the steaming water to a boil on high heat and steam until the pudding is firm (about 20 minutes).
TO SERVE	Chill thoroughly. Loosen pudding from mold by shaking with a quick, circular wrist motion. Place a shallow bowl over the top of the mold and quickly turn upside down. Be sure to get all the caramel out of the bottom of the mold. Pour chilled canned fruit salad, fruit cocktail, or other in-season fruit over the top.

CANDIED WINTER MELON

This delicacy can often be bought in oriental groceries, but can be made at home fresh, too. Naturally, the type made at home is considered much prettier and better. This is usually made at New Years time, when it is cool, because you need to keep an eye on it while it cooks. It is often cooked in a large copper kettle, over a charcoal fire. Many people consider this confection a real challenge, since winter melon is one of the most tender of all vegetables, and to be able to cook it for a long enough period to make it into a confection sounds impossible.

5-lb. winter melon

Buy an older, tougher melon instead of a young tender one, if possible. Peel the melon and remove the pithy inner section with the seeds. Discard peel and pith. Cut the firm, white outside meat into strips at least ½ inch thick, about 1 inch wide and from 2 to 4 inches long. The strips will shrink during cooking.

1 tbsp. slaked lime (calcium hydroxide, available from the druggist)
12 cups water
Large pot

(If you prefer, just buy a gallon or so of lime water from your druggist.) Put the powdered calcium hydroxide and the water in a large pot. Stir well to mix, then dump in the pieces of melon. Let soak for one hour. This will give a slightly crunchy texture to the final product.

Drain off the lime water and rinse the melon thoroughly under cool running water.

2 tbsp. alum
12 cups water

Pound the alum into a fine powder. Mix it with the water, making certain there is enough liquid to cover the winter melon pieces. Put the melon in and let soak overnight. This soaking in alum water makes the final product firm. Otherwise, the winter melon would get mushy after cooking it more than 15 minutes.

Next day, drain the alum water from the melon pieces and, without rinsing, cover with fresh water. Bring to a boil and cook about 4 or 5 minutes on medium heat.

Drain the melon again, and this time rinse very very well under cool running water. Drain and wash several times, to be sure all the traces of alum water are removed. The alum also has a tendency to make the confection turn yellow, if the heat gets a little too high.

Electric skillet
4 cups sugar

If an extra-large electric skillet is available, it may be possible to cook all the melon pieces at the same time. If not, divide in half and cook two batches. (Or halve the recipe?) Mix the sugar and the melon pieces together and put into the electric skillet. Set the temperature at 250 F and cook about 20 minutes. Turn the pieces and move them about frequently (gently, gently) using chopsticks, tongs, or a spoon. Water will begin to come out of the melon, lots of syrupy juice will form, and the pieces will begin shrinking.

Increase the heat to 300 F and continue to cook about 10 minutes. This is when it is important to watch closely to keep the confection from turning yellow. Turn each piece frequently to allow proper drainage and equal contact with the heat for each piece.

Reduce the heat to 250 F once more and continue to cook, turning the pieces occasionally, until the juice has almost all been absorbed. There should still be a covering of syrup over the bottom of the pan.

Reduce the heat to 200 F and cook until all the juice is absorbed. Don't rush it—the total cooking time will be 3 or 4 hours. If you try to cook it too fast, the pieces will turn yellowish and will not be nearly so pretty. The color should be almost clear, and the pieces will be almost transparent.

TO SERVE   Serve as a candy, or use in cake (see page 99).

FRESH ORANGE CONFECTION   *Four (or more) servings*

This light and refreshing dessert is as lovely to look at as it is to eat.

4 navel oranges (large)   Shave off a thin layer of the outer skin, leaving half or more of the inner part of the skin intact. The orange should still have an orange tint to it—don't peel away to the white pith inside.

Make six deep slits lengthwise in the skin of the orange, cutting deep into the inside, starting about one inch from the stem end and running to within about one inch of the navel end.

Large pot
Water to cover   Put the oranges into the pot and cover with water. Bring to a boil and continue boiling on medium heat for 30 minutes. This makes the pulp tender.

Drain the oranges, and submerge in cold water to cool off. When cooled, poke with a sharp knife around through the side slits to loosen the pith and pulp. Slowly and gently press the top of each orange until the slits widen and the orange begins to flatten. Gently, with the fingers, pull out the extra pulp and pith that appears between the sides of each slit. Continue to press until the oranges are only 1½ to 2 inches high. The slits will be fairly wide, and much of the pulp will be discarded. Leave some of the pulp inside.

1 tsp. alum
Water to cover   Place the oranges again in the saucepan, with water to cover. Mix in the alum, which will keep the orange rind firm so it will not disintegrate during the following cooking. Bring to a boil on high heat, then lower the heat to medium and boil for another 30 minutes.

Drain off the hot alum water, and once more cool the oranges in cold water. When cool, press firmly to drain, then let drain in a colander or on a cake cooler grid for about 5 minutes.

2 cups sugar
¾ cup water   Put the oranges into the saucepan once more, pour the sugar over them, then pour the water over all. Bring to a boil quickly on high heat, then reduce the heat to low. Let the oranges simmer slowly until the syrup has almost completely disappeared. Turn the oranges over occasionally, using great care not to tear them.

TO SERVE   Serve cool. May be sliced into small portions, or for those who know about these oranges serve one for each individual. These can be refrigerated for two or three months if kept in a tightly sealed container. Can also be frozen.

HORS D'OEUVRES

THESE RECIPES are not necessarily used as hors d'oeuvres in Vietnam, but have been found to serve especially well in that guise among foreigners. All of these recipes may also be served as one of several or even as the main course at a regular meal.

FRIED SHRIMP PATTIES

This is good as an hors-d'oeuvre, as a light luncheon with lettuce, or may be served as the main dish with rice, soup, and salad.

1 clove garlic *Dash of pepper* *1 lb. Shrimp Paste*	Mash and chop the garlic clove fine. Add it into the basic SHRIMP PASTE (page 25), then add pepper and continue to knead until thoroughly mixed in.
Deep-fat fryer or *heavy skillet* *1-inch cooking oil*	Form the Shrimp Paste into small patties about ½ inch thick, 3 or 4 inches across, and drop into hot oil. Fry quickly on medium high heat until brown on both sides (about 2 or 3 minutes).
TO SERVE	Serve piping hot with rice, NUOC MAM SAUCE (page 23), leaf lettuce, mint, and Chinese parsley, if served as a main dish. Serve piping hot with a side dish of Nuoc Mam Sauce and a platter of leaf lettuce and mint to wrap the patties, if served as hors-d'oeuvres.

BARBECUED SHRIMP PATTIES

2 cloves garlic *2 tbsp. fat or cooking* *oil* *¼ tsp. pepper* *2 lbs. Shrimp Paste*	Mash and chop the garlic fine. Add garlic, fat or cooking oil, and pepper to the BASIC SHRIMP PASTE (page 25). Knead until thoroughly mixed. Set aside.
Barbecue stove and *rack* *Charcoal*	Make fire.
	Shape the Shrimp Paste into small patties about ½ inch thick, and 3 or 4 inches across. Place the shrimp patties on the rack and put it over burning charcoal. Barbecue until brown on both sides.
TO SERVE	Serve hot. Wrap in lettuce leaves, including mint leaves, and dip in a side dish of NUOC MAM SAUCE (page 23).

STEAMED SHRIMP LOAF

Four servings

This makes a very good hors d'oeuvre, served either hot or cold. It is also a good main dish, served with rice and salad.

Steamer pan *2 fresh ti leaves or a* * fresh banana leaf* * (substitute: cloth)* *Cooking oil*	See page 10 for a description of the steamer and the general procedure for its use. Wash the leaves, dry with a paper towel or dish towel, and oil slightly. Place the leaves in the top section of the steamer pan as a lining over the holes in the bottom. A piece of closely woven cloth such as a tea towel may be oiled and used as a substitute, if the leaves are not available. Leaves are used in Vietnam as the most practical thing. They are discarded after use.
Shrimp Paste	Pat out the SHRIMP PASTE (page 25) on the leaves in a flat round cake about ½ inch thick. Add cold water to the bottom section of the steamer, set the top in place with the shrimp cake inside, and cover. After the water comes to a boil, begin timing. Steam, on high heat, for about 7 or 8 minutes (just until firm). There will probably be a small residue of liquid on top of the loaf. Blot this up with a paper towel, being careful not to get a steam burn on your hand or arm.
1 egg yolk	Use the yolk of the egg left over when making the shrimp paste. Beat yolk slightly and spread over the top of the hot shrimp loaf with a pastry brush. Let stand, uncovered, in the steamer until egg yolk is slightly firm. Do not cover. If it is covered, the yolk gets too hard and the smell is "eggy."
TO SERVE	Remove shrimp loaf to a plate and slice into squares. Serve hot or cold, with NUOC MAM SAUCE (page 23). If served as a main dish, it should be accompanied by steamed rice, a salad, and a soup.

SHRIMP ON TOAST

This is a delicious hors d'oeuvre or a luncheon eaten with lettuce, mint, Chinese parsley, and sliced cucumbers.

1 lb. Shrimp Paste *¼ tsp. pepper*	Add pepper to the SHRIMP PASTE (page 25) and mix well.
Thin-sliced bread	For this recipe two- or three-day-old bread is best. Cut the bread into rounds or squares, of a size that can be easily managed as an hors-d'oeuvre. Spread the Shrimp Paste on one side of the bread, in whatever thickness you like.
Deep fat fryer or * heavy skillet* *2 inches of cooking* * oil*	Heat oil and fry the Shrimp on Toast until brown. Fry the shrimp-side down first, then the bread side.
TO SERVE	Serve hot. Wrap Shrimp on Toast in lettuce with mint, Chinese parsley, and a side dish of NUOC MAM SAUCE (page 23) for dipping.

STEAMED FISH LOAF

Begin with the basic recipe for FISH PASTE (page 25), and continue as below. This is good as hors d'oeuvres, or may be used as a main dish for a light meal.

2 cloves garlic *2 lb. Fish Paste* *Dash of black pepper*	Chop and crush the garlic cloves. Add to the Fish Paste with the black pepper and continue to knead and squeeze until mixed in thoroughly.
Steamer *Ti leaves, banana leaf,* *or oiled cloth*	Line the steamer top with leaves or with a piece of closely-woven cloth which has been well saturated with cooking oil, so that the holes are covered. See page 10 for detailed instructions on using a steamer. Pat the fish paste out into a flat, round cake about 1 inch thick and place on top of the leaves. Place in the steamer top, over boiling water in the steamer bottom, and cover. Steam, over high heat, 6 to 8 minutes, just until firm. The fish loaf will turn whiter. Turn off heat, and remove the cover. Excess liquid will have collected on top of the fish loaf and it should be carefully blotted off with a paper towel. Be careful not to get a steam burn.
1 egg yolk *Pastry brush*	Use the egg yolk left over when making the Fish Paste. Stir the yolk just until mixed, and brush all of it onto the top of the fish loaf. Let the loaf remain in the steamer, uncovered, just until the yolk sets. Do not cover again, or the yolk will get too hard and take on an unpleasant eggy taste. Remove steamer from heat and allow to cool off for a few minutes.
TO SERVE	This may be served hot or cold, and is very good served as a hot hors d'oeuvre since it will also be tasty when it gets cooled off! Slice into 1-inch squares to serve. It should be served with a side dish of NUOC MAM SAUCE (page 23) for dipping the squares. This may also be served as a main dish, with a soup, salad and rice.

FRIED FISH LOAF ON TOAST

This is an especially good hot hors d'oeuvre.

2 cloves garlic *2 lb. Fish Paste*	Chop and mash the garlic fine. Add to the basic FISH PASTE (page 25), kneading until thoroughly mixed in.
Thin-sliced bread	Cut the bread into rounds or squares, of a size that can be easily managed as an hors d'oeuvre. Spread the fish paste on one side of the bread, in whatever thickness you like. You'd probably better experiment a little to begin with, before the guests begin to arrive.

Deep fat fryer, or
   deep skillet
2 inches of cooking oil
   in fryer or skillet
	Heat the oil and fry the fish-on-toast. Fry with the fish side down first, then the bread side.

TO SERVE	Serve wrapped in leaf lettuce, with mint, Chinese parsley, and a side dish of NUOC MAM SAUCE (page 23) for dipping.

FRIED FISH PATTIES

This is good as an accompaniment to a heavier meal, as an hors d'oeuvre, as a light luncheon with lettuce, or may be served as the main dish with rice, soup, and salad.

2 cloves garlic *2 lb. Fish Paste*	Mash and chop the garlic cloves fine. Add to the basic FISH PASTE recipe (page 25) and continue to knead until thoroughly mixed in.
Deep fat fryer *2 inches cooking oil*	Form the paste into small cakes about ½ inch thick, 3 or 4 inches across, and drop into hot oil. Fry quickly, on medium to medium high heat until brown on both sides (about 2 or 3 minutes).
TO SERVE	Serve piping hot with rice, NUOC MAM SAUCE (page 23) and leaf lettuce, if used as a main dish or as an accompaniment to a meal. Serve piping hot, with a side dish of Nuoc Mam Sauce and a platter of leaf lettuce to wrap pieces of the cake in, if served as an hors d'oeuvre.

PORK CHEESE

Some people object to the basic idea of eating pig's head. Just don't tell them what they're eating and they will probably enjoy it very much! Makes a good hors d'oeuvre, and is good for dieters. It is also easy to carry on a picnic.

⅓ cup (loose pack) *dried tree fungus* *Hot water to cover*	In a 2-quart container, put the pieces of dried tree fungus (see page 20) to soak in hot water, for at least one hour. The pieces will expand considerably, and will resemble black, thin, mushrooms. When soft, cut the very large pieces in half and remove the stems or any black specks where the fungus was growing onto the tree.
½ small pig's head, *boned*	Ask the butcher to give you half a head, cleaned and boned, It should have one ear and half the snout, and should have the skin still on. Wash the head well, and clean off any remaining bristles that you can easily get off. It will be easier to get the head completely cleaned of bristles after it cooks a little while, in the next step. Cut into 3 or 4 pieces.
Large pot *Water*	Put the pieces in the pot and cover with cold water. Cover pot, bring to a boil, and cook on high heat about 30 minutes.
	Drain head meat in a colander, and rinse well under running cold water to clean and cool. Cut in small pieces, not larger than ¼ × 2 × 3 inches, cutting the ear into narrow strips, and removing any remaining small bones. Also finish cleaning off any remaining bristles. Some people prefer less fat, so the excess fat should be removed at this point if you don't want it. Be sure to include the ears, skin, and snout. That is what makes the cheese jell.

2 large shallots (or
  white part of green
  onions)
1 tbsp. cooking oil
Large skillet
	Slice shallots in very thin rounds. Heat the oil in a large skillet, and saute the shallots for a few seconds, until the odor begins to rise. Add the pieces of tree fungus and head meat, reduce the heat to medium and saute, stirring, about 3 minutes.

1½ tsp. peppercorns	Add the whole peppercorns, stir, and continue to cook on medium heat another 2 minutes. This gives a nice spicy flavor, and is also decorative.
1½ tbsp. fish sauce	Add fish sauce, stir well and cook, stirring, for 1 minute. Remove from heat.
Bag made of cheesecloth or other loosely woven cloth (about 10 to 12 inches long, 3 or 4 inches across)	At this step, in Vietnam, the mixture is wrapped in a ti leaf or banana leaf and tied firmly. These leaves have no particular taste of their own and are very sturdy. It takes much practice and dexterity to do this alone. A cloth bag will serve the same purpose, and can be made at home. Stuff the meat mixture into the bag, pressing it down into the bag so it is packed very, very tight. When all is stuffed into the bag, tie the top or make the bag with a drawstring, and hang it up to drip. Place it over a pan or other container to catch the greasy drip. There will be very little drip, actually; and the drip will jell into strings almost like icicles on the bottom of the bag.
	When thoroughly cooled, place into plastic bag (cloth bag and all), or aluminum foil, to keep it from drying out. Put this package into a loaf or other small pan, and put a heavy weight on top, to press the mixture together more firmly. Chill in refrigerator at least three hours before serving. It should be firmly jelled, about the consistency of pressed ham.
TO SERVE	Unwrap, remove the cloth bag, and cut in 1-inch slices. Cut each slice into quarters or sixths. Serve cold, as hors d'oeuvres. Best served with a side dish of NUOC MAM SAUCE (page 23) as a dip. May also be served as a light luncheon, with steamed rice, leaf lettuce, and Nuoc Mam Sauce.

STEAMED BUNS

Yield: two dozen

Here is another kind of bun that is good party fare, but is also an exceptionally good meal in itself.

FILLING	
3 dried mushrooms *10 dried lily flowers (optional)* *Warm water to cover*	Soak the dried mushrooms and lily flowers together in warm water to cover until soft (about 15 minutes). Cut away the stem portion of the mushrooms and discard. Discard the hard end of the lily flower stem. Chop all very fine.
Piece of bamboo shoot (part of a can, optional) *1 shallot (or 1 small onion)* *5 or 6 fresh (frozen) shrimp, shelled*	Drain the bamboo shoot. Be sure to use the Chinese kind, because of the flavor. Chop the bamboo shoot, shallot, and shrimp very fine.
⅓ lb. lean ground pork *¼ tsp. salt* *Dash of black pepper* *2 tbsp. cooking oil* *Large heavy skillet*	Heat the cooking oil in the heavy skillet on medium high heat. Put in the ground pork, salt, pepper, chopped mushroom, lily flowers, bamboo shoot, shallot, and shrimp. Saute, stirring constantly, on medium high heat about 5 minutes.
1 tsp. fish sauce	Add the fish sauce, stir, and remove from heat. Set aside to cool.

109

DOUGH

1½ cups rice flour
½ cup potato flour
1 egg white
1 tsp. salt
¾ cup water
1 tsp. cooking oil

Mix the egg white, salt, oil, and water together, beating well with a fork. Mix the two kinds of flour in a large bowl. Pour in the water and egg mixture and mix well. Knead, when it gets stiff. Put on a lightly floured board and roll out. Fold the dough over several times to make a ball of the dough, and roll out again. Repeat this folding and rolling process 5 or 6 times.

Roll out the dough as thin as possible. Cut into circles 3 or 4 inches across. Use a large cookie cutter or a cup, saucer, or other round item, cutting around the edge with a very sharp knife.

Place 1 teaspoonful of filling in the center, slightly to one side of each circle. Fold the circle of dough in half over the filling and crimp the edges closed, using the fingers or a fork. This makes a flat- and fat-bottomed half-circle.

Steamer (page 10)

Place hot water in the bottom section of the steamer. Put the buns in the top section, standing each bun on its flat side, with the crimped half-circle edge pointing up. Put the top section of the steamer in place over the bottom, cover, and steam on high heat about 30 minutes.

TO SERVE

Serve hot, or warm. May be reheated in the steamer. If desired, make a supply ahead and freeze them. Thaw before reheating. Good served with NUOC MAM SAUCE (page 23) as a dip.

LITTLE STUFFED BUNS

This is very good as an hors d'oeuvre, but may also be served with a dinner as an accompaniment.

1 cup flour
3 tbsp. shortening (lard)

Cut in shortening as for pie dough. Lard is used in Vietnam, because it is more available and because the flavor is preferred.

1 egg

Add the egg. Mix well, and knead several times. Roll out, fold over, and roll out again. Repeat this rolling and folding 5 or 6 times.

STUFFING

½ lb. boiled lean pork (page 23)

Slice, then cut into very fine strips, then cut into smaller pieces (about ⅛-inch cubes, or smaller).

5 dried mushrooms
Water to cover

Soak mushrooms 15 minutes in warm water to cover. Chop very fine (same size as meat particles).

1 small onion

Chop into fine pieces, same size as meat and mushrooms.

2 or 3 water chestnuts
2 tbsp. almonds

Chop water chestnuts and almonds into fine pieces, same size as other ingredients.

1 tsp. oil
Medium skillet

Mix everything together, heat the oil and saute the mixture, stirring, about 1 minute on medium high heat.

¼ tsp. salt
1 tbsp. fish sauce
Dash of black pepper

Mix the salt, fish sauce, and pepper into the mixture in the skillet, stir well, and cook about 3 more minutes on medium heat. Set aside to cool.

Back to the dough. Roll it as thin as possible. Paper thin, if you can. Cut in approximately 3-inch squares.

Put a teaspoon of the meat mixture in the center of each square. To fold up: First fold the third that is toward you over the meat. Then fold the opposite side over. This will make an oblong roll. Press the ends closed. Then fold each end in toward the center.

TO BAKE Preheat oven to 350 F. Place the buns on a cookie sheet and bake about 30 minutes, or until golden brown.

TO FRY Fry in deep fat, a few at a time, until golden brown.

These can be kept warm in the oven until served. Can be frozen, and reheated in the oven after thawing.

STUFFED BREAD *A baker's dozen*

This stuffed bread is the Vietnamese version of an Asian favorite that was perhaps originally Chinese. This dough is lighter than the usual, and the stuffing a little tastier. It is easy to make this ahead of time in large quantities, and freeze for future use. To freeze, be sure to steam the dough first. When removing from the freezer, put the frozen buns into the steamer and steam about 20 minutes, or until soft.

THE DOUGH Scald the milk, then set aside to cool until it is lukewarm.
¾ cup milk

⅓ cup lukewarm water Mix the sugar and water; add the yeast and let it soak at least
¼ tsp. sugar 5 minutes. Then add the milk.
¾ tsp. dried yeast

3 cups flour Sift the flour, salt, and sugar together. Add the flour mixture to
¼ tsp. salt the milk and yeast mixture and mix well.
1 tsp. sugar

1 tbsp. shortening Melt the shortening and mix into the dough. Stir until the dough forms a ball, then put out onto a lightly floured board and knead until elastic (about 5 or 10 minutes). Form the dough into a ball that should be soft but not sticky.

Medium-size bowl Put the dough into a clean bowl and cover with a damp cloth.
Cloth to cover Put it in a warm place (about 85° F.) until it doubles in bulk, taking probably 2 or 3 hours, or it can be left overnight to rise, if desired.

Punch the dough down and knead for only 2 or 3 minutes. Put it back in the warm place for 20 or 30 minutes more, after which it should be ready to use.

THE STUFFING Soak the dried shrimp in warm water to cover for about 15
3 tbsp. dried shrimp minutes. Chop fine. (This is optional—many people prefer to
  (optional) omit or to substitute a few pieces of fresh shrimp.)
Warm water to cover

111

½ lb. lean ground pork
2 shallots (or white
    part of green onions)
2 Chinese sausages
½ tsp. salt
Dash of monosodium
    glutamate

Slice the shallots in very thin rounds. Slice the Chinese sausages thin, at an angle. Mix the ground pork, shallots, sliced sausages, salt, and monosodium glutamate. Then add the finely chopped shrimp. Mix all together well.

1 tbsp. fish sauce

Mix the fish sauce in, and set aside until the dough is ready to be stuffed.

STUFFING VARIATION
2 tbsp. cooking oil
Heavy skillet

Some people prefer to saute the stuffing before putting it into the middle of the dough. If you wish to try it, preheat the oil, and saute the stuffing mix for 2 or 3 minutes on high heat, stirring constantly.

TO PREPARE
13 squares white paper
    (3 × 3 inches)

Punch the dough down again. Pinch off an egg-sized lump of the dough and roll gently between the hands to make a ball. Then flatten and spread with the hands, into a circle about 4 inches across. Put a heaping teaspoonful of the stuffing in the center of the circle, pull the sides up and fold over and pinch together to close; pat with the fingers to make a smooth ball. Put the pinched-together side down on a square of white paper. Let the buns raise another 15 or 20 minutes before steaming.

Steamer (see page 10)

Put water in the bottom section of the steamer, and place on high heat. In the upper section, place 4 buns (or 5, or 6, depending on the size of your steamer). They will increase in size so leave at least one inch between buns. Cover the upper section of the steamer. Let the buns steam on high heat until done (about 15 minutes).

TO SERVE

Serve hot or cold. Good as a complete meal, with a little salad or soup. Wonderful to take along on a picnic.

INDEX

113

117